Cambridge Elements

Elements in Politics and Society in East Asia
edited by
Erin Aeran Chung
Johns Hopkins University
Mary Alice Haddad
Wesleyan University
Benjamin L. Read
University of California, Santa Cruz

U.S. ALLIES AND THE TAIWAN STRAIT

Adam P. Liff
Indiana University

Shaftesbury Road, Cambridge CB2 8EA, United Kingdom

One Liberty Plaza, 20th Floor, New York, NY 10006, USA

477 Williamstown Road, Port Melbourne, VIC 3207, Australia

314–321, 3rd Floor, Plot 3, Splendor Forum, Jasola District Centre, New Delhi – 110025, India

103 Penang Road, #05–06/07, Visioncrest Commercial, Singapore 238467

Cambridge University Press is part of Cambridge University Press & Assessment, a department of the University of Cambridge.

We share the University's mission to contribute to society through the pursuit of education, learning and research at the highest international levels of excellence.

www.cambridge.org
Information on this title: www.cambridge.org/9781009644228
DOI: 10.1017/9781009405638

© Adam P. Liff 2025

This publication is in copyright. Subject to statutory exception and to the provisions of relevant collective licensing agreements, with the exception of the Creative Commons version the link for which is provided below, no reproduction of any part may take place without the written permission of Cambridge University Press & Assessment.

An online version of this work is published at doi.org/10.1017/9781009405638 under a Creative Commons Open Access license CC-BY-NC-ND 4.0 which permits re-use, distribution and reproduction in any medium for non-commercial purposes providing appropriate credit to the original work is given. You may not distribute derivative works without permission. To view a copy of this license, visit https://creativecommons.org/licenses/by-nc-nd/4.0

When citing this work, please include a reference to the DOI 10.1017/9781009405638

First published 2025

A catalogue record for this publication is available from the British Library

ISBN 978-1-009-64422-8 Hardback
ISBN 978-1-009-40566-9 Paperback
ISSN 2632-7368 (online)
ISSN 2632-735X (print)

Cambridge University Press & Assessment has no responsibility for the persistence or accuracy of URLs for external or third-party internet websites referred to in this publication and does not guarantee that any content on such websites is, or will remain, accurate or appropriate.

For EU product safety concerns, contact us at Calle de José Abascal, 56, 1°, 28003 Madrid, Spain, or email eugpsr@cambridge.org

U.S. Allies and the Taiwan Strait

Elements in Politics and Society in East Asia

DOI: 10.1017/9781009405638
First published online: December 2025

Adam P. Liff
Indiana University
Author for correspondence: Adam P. Liff, aliff@iu.edu

Abstract: Against the backdrop of worsening tensions across the Taiwan Strait, this Element analyzes the positions and policies vis-à-vis Taiwan of six major democratic U.S. treaty allies—Japan, Australia, South Korea, the United Kingdom, France, Germany—and the European Union. Historically and today, these U.S. partners have exercised far greater agency supporting Taiwan's international space and cross-Strait stability—in key instances even blazing early trails Washington would later follow—than the overwhelmingly U.S.-centric academic and policy discourse generally suggests. Decades ago, each crafted an intentionally ambiguous official position regarding Taiwan's status that effectively granted subsequent political leaders considerable flexibility to operationalize their government's "One China" policy and officially "unofficial" relationship with Taiwan. Today, intensifying cross-Strait frictions ensure that U.S. allies' policy choices will remain critical factors affecting the status quo's sustainability and democratic Taiwan's continued viability as an autonomous international actor. This title is also available as Open Access on Cambridge Core.

Keywords: U.S. alliances, Taiwan, One China, East Asia, Europe

© Adam P. Liff 2025

ISBNs: 9781009644228 (HB), 9781009405669 (PB), 9781009405638 (OC)
ISSNs: 2632-7368 (online), 2632-735X (print)

Contents

1 Introduction   1

2 "One China" and the Taiwan Strait: The Distinction between Beijing's "Principle" and the U.S. and Allies' "Policies"   12

3 Indo-Pacific Allies: Japan, South Korea, and Australia   28

4 European Allies and Partners: The UK, France, Germany, the EU, and NATO   44

5 Discussion and Major Takeaways   70

6 Conclusion   81

References   88

1 Introduction

On August 3, 2022, the People's Liberation Army (PLA), the military of the Chinese Communist Party (CCP), commenced its largest-ever live-fire exercises around self-governed, democratic Taiwan. Amid the worst cross-Strait frictions in decades, with relations between the United States and the People's Republic of China (PRC; below "China") at a post-normalization nadir, and just six months after Russia's invasion of Ukraine and announcement of a "no limits partnership" with Beijing, China's seemingly disproportionate response to a U.S. House Speaker's peaceful visit to a long-standing U.S. democratic and economic partner sent shockwaves around the world.

In the two years since, Beijing's normalization of unprecedented or previously rare military and other actions designed to "punish" Taiwan's democratically elected leaders has undermined the decades-old cross-Strait status quo and exacerbated long-standing fears of a potential conflict. Of particular concern are the PLA's now regular crossings of the unofficial median line dividing the Strait, large aerial and naval maneuvers around Taiwan, and simulated joint precision strikes involving China's aircraft carriers.

Beijing's unprecedentedly large-scale military exercises since summer 2022 – including similarly massive exercises around Taiwan in April 2023 and May 2024 – are intended not only as valuable training opportunities for the PLA and to send coercive signals to leaders in Taipei. They are also designed to demonstrate to foreign audiences the rapidly modernizing and expanding PLA's ability to encircle Taiwan; to blockade its trade-dependent economy, potentially as the opening phase of an invasion; and to complicate potential U.S. efforts to come to the rescue. This is in addition to increasing concerns about "gray zone" coercion, including activities by China's coast guard – the world's largest.

More fundamentally, however, Beijing's recent escalation of rhetoric and provocative maneuvers are intended to send a political signal: to demonstrate the seriousness of the PRC's claim of sovereignty over Taiwan based on its self-defined "one-China principle" (*yi ge Zhongguo yuanze*). That signal has not been lost in foreign capitals; in 2023, U.S. CIA Director William Burns publicly confirmed that Xi Jinping, the PRC's paramount leader, has ordered the PLA to "be ready by 2027" to seize Taiwan. Importantly, he also noted that fact alone "doesn't mean that conflict is imminent or inevitable" (CIA.gov 2023).

In short, although the PRC has never governed Taiwan Beijing is determined to "unify" Taiwan with the mainland – by force, if necessary. In stark contrast, and although views in democratic Taiwan concerning the island's relationship with "China" are contested (see Section 2), no major political party there accepts Beijing's contention that Taiwan is part of, or subordinate to, the CCP-led PRC (Chen 2022). For their parts, President Tsai Ing-wen (2016–2024) and her successor William Lai (2024–) – both from Taiwan's left-of-center Democratic Progressive Party (DPP) – maintain that the democratic "Republic of China Taiwan" is already a "sovereign" and "independent nation." (Zhonghua Minguo Zongtongfu 2020; 2024). Aware that any move toward a de jure declaration of independence could provoke a conflict, however, as president both also expressed a commitment to maintain the status quo – the preference of the overwhelming majority of Taiwan's voters.

1.1 Internationalizing Concerns amid the Increasingly Precarious Status Quo

Since the DPP's return to the presidency in 2016, PRC leaders have repeatedly called Taiwan's leaders "separatists." Beijing has employed increasingly diverse economic, diplomatic, and political tools to pressure Taiwan, including efforts to shrink its "international space." These measures include suspending official cross-Strait communication channels, getting nine of Taiwan's few remaining official diplomatic allies to switch recognition from the ROC to the PRC, exerting economic and diplomatic pressure on Taiwan's international partners (even subnational governments, businesses, and civil society groups), and cutting off Taiwan's already limited access to international organizations, even to those with which Taipei was previously able to engage (e.g., the World Health Organization).

In short, the global headline-generating, unprecedentedly large-scale PLA maneuvers each of the past three years are but the most conspicuous evidence of a new, more potentially incendiary normal in Beijing's efforts to assert its 75-year-old sovereignty claim, and to weaken international support for Taiwan. Summing up the years-long trend in the weeks after the PLA's August 2022 exercises, U.S. Secretary of State Antony Blinken highlighted a "change in the approach from Beijing toward Taiwan," including "a fundamental decision that the status quo was no longer acceptable and that Beijing was determined to pursue reunification on a much faster timeline" (*Washington Post* 2022). This assessment came nearly a year after Biden's Pentagon had already identified "a Taiwan contingency" as its "pacing scenario" (Ratner 2021). Against this precarious backdrop and following the DPP's victory in January 2024's presidential election – its third in a row – the possibility of a peaceful, uncoerced resolution of the cross-Strait dispute appears increasingly remote.

Recognizing this reality, as well as the changing balances of power across the Strait and wider region, an important feature of the Biden administration's Asia policy has been an unprecedentedly proactive effort to enlist key democratic U.S. allies and partners in a coordinated campaign to publicly emphasize "the importance of peace and stability across the Taiwan Strait as an indispensable element in security and prosperity in the international community," and to call for both "peaceful resolution of cross-Strait issues" and Taiwan's "meaningful participation" in international organizations (e.g., G7 2023a). This effort is consistent with Biden's more general emphases on the importance of U.S. alliances – which he identified in his first major foreign policy speech as the U.S.' "greatest asset" – and the need "to rally the nations of the world to defend democracy globally [and] to push back ... authoritarianism's advance" (White House 2021a). It also reflects a sober judgment that the global fallout from any conflict across the Taiwan Strait would be profound. As an early signal to even geographically distant allies and partners of the wide-ranging stakes, the U.S. National Security Council's top Indo-Pacific official stressed that a conflict would "broaden quickly and ... fundamentally trash the global economy" (*Nikkei Asia* 2021).

1.2 High Stakes in the Taiwan Strait

From Beijing's perspective, the question of how to settle Taiwan's ambiguous international status and incorporate it into the PRC – the heart of the "One China" issue – has long been the most fundamental in China's foreign and security policy. Seventy-five years after the PRC's 1949 establishment, its leaders continue to identify Taiwan as being "at the heart of China's core interests." They identify "resolving the Taiwan question and realizing China's complete reunification" as "indispensable for the realization of China's rejuvenation" and the CCP's "historic mission." And they have long asserted that the cross-Strait dispute is "purely an internal matter for China," regularly warning Washington and others that "the Taiwan question is growing into the biggest risk in China-U.S. relations," one that "if mishandled could severely damage bilateral ties" (State Council 2022; Wang 2022).

Global reactions to the recent worsening of cross-Strait frictions demonstrate that U.S. government is not alone in expressing its concerns about these trends, and about Taiwan more generally. As detailed in Sections 3 and 4, many other U.S. allies' leaders – especially in the Western Pacific and Europe – have become increasingly outspoken about their nations' interests in continued peace and stability across the Taiwan Strait, as well as their support for Taiwan's international space. There is also more general recognition of the potentially catastrophic implications of a war or coerced resolution to the cross-Strait dispute for Taiwan's twenty-three million people and its nearly one million foreign residents.

Also attracting unprecedented attention in foreign capitals have been the potentially immense global economic consequences of a Taiwan Strait contingency. Roughly 50 percent of global container traffic flows through the Taiwan Strait daily. Taiwan is the world's sixteenth largest trading economy, a technological powerhouse, and the source of the vast majority of the world's most advanced semiconductors. It is also a top-ten trading partner of the United States and a top-five trading partner of China, Japan, and South Korea. For these reasons, one widely referenced 2022 analysis estimates that even a non-kinetic blockade of Taiwan – that is, one not involving direct physical or deadly force – would cause "well over two trillion dollars" in global economic disruption, "even before factoring in international responses or second-order effects" (emphasis added). It concludes that the consequences "would be felt immediately and ... difficult to reverse" (Vest, Kratz, and Goujon 2022).

If the crisis were to escalate, possibly to involve direct conflict between China and the United States, the regional and global fallout could be even more catastrophic. A 2024 *Bloomberg* analysis estimated that the global economy would suffer a $5 trillion hit if the PRC blockaded Taiwan, whereas a shooting war would deal a $10 trillion blow – an amount equivalent to 10 percent of global GDP and which would dwarf the impact of both the 2009 Global Financial Crisis and 2020 COVID-19 pandemic (*Bloomberg* 2024a).

1.3 Beyond the U.S.-PRC-Taiwan "Triangle"

Behind these estimates is a widespread expectation that Washington, for many decades Taiwan's most important international partner and de facto security guarantor, is unlikely to stand idly by if a cross-Strait crisis were to escalate. As summarized in Section 2, Washington's long-standing official policy holds that Taiwan's status remains "undetermined" and the cross-Strait dispute must be resolved peacefully through dialogue. Furthermore, while U.S. policy leaves ambiguous how it would respond if China attacked Taiwan, a 1979 law obligates the government to provide defensive arms to Taiwan and maintain the U.S. ability to "resist" any use of force or coercion that threatens Taiwan's security, inter alia ("Taiwan Relations Act" 1979).

Though the United States is undoubtedly Taiwan's most significant international partner, the urgency with which the Biden administration has sought to more robustly engage U.S. allies in support of Taiwan reflects increasingly mainstream recognition of their agency and significance, especially against the backdrop of China's rapidly expanding military capabilities and diplomatic and economic influence. For example, Blinken warned Beijing that U.S. allies would "take action [if Beijing seeks] to use force to disrupt the status quo"

(*Reuters* 2021a). At the 2023 G7 summit, Biden himself stated that "We're going to continue to put Taiwan in a position that they can defend themselves. And there is clear understanding among most of our allies that, in fact, if China were to act unilaterally, there would be a response" (White House 2023a).

In response to these developments and as an apparent effort to preemptively deter such an outcome, throughout 2024 Beijing issued a series of thinly veiled threats against U.S. allies. For example, in April remarks that echoed comments in other allied capitals from Chinese diplomats, PRC Ambassador to Japan Wu Jianghao told a Japanese audience: "If Japan ties itself to the tanks plotting to split China, the Japanese people will be brought into the fire. These are painful words to hear, but they need to be clearly stated. The Japanese should not say that they were not informed in advance" (PRC Embassy Japan 2024).

Against the backdrop of a rapidly changing balance of power, high-profile assertions by U.S. leaders that U.S. allies would respond in a crisis, and the increased frequency and volume of rhetorical backlash from Beijing, it is important for academic and policy debates regarding the Taiwan Strait to move beyond the U.S.-centric bias and narrow focus on the U.S.-PRC-Taiwan triangle that has long dominated. In particular, it is necessary to devote greater attention to major democratic U.S. treaty allies' agency and the impact that their diverse histories, positions, and policies have had on Taiwan's international space, cross-Strait peace and stability, and the effective meaning of "One China" in international politics.

1.4 Countering the Spread of Dis/misinformation

The decades-old U.S.-centric bias is a concern not only for the academic literature but also for the health of front-burner political and policy debates in Washington and allied capitals today. As highlighted in Section 2, widespread unfamiliarity with the history and subtleties of issues related to Taiwan and the Taiwan Strait among new generations of leaders has enabled Beijing's disinformation campaigns – which typically ignore the nuances and intentional ambiguities of the U.S. and key allies' respective "One China" policies in favor of a narrative falsely claiming a "universal consensus" about its claim of sovereignty over Taiwan – to find strikingly fertile ground in which to take root. For example, Beijing frequently attempts to unilaterally define for the United States and its major allies what their respective positions on Taiwan's status are, as well as what words or actions constitute a "violation" of their alleged past "commitments." More generally, it promotes revisionist histories of United Nations Resolution 2758 (1971), which granted "China's" seat to representatives from the PRC, falsely asserting that this resolution was somehow the final word from the international community on Taiwan's legal status or whether it is part of China. It was not. In fact, the text of the resolution does not even mention "Taiwan" or "the Republic of China" (Drun and Glaser 2022).

Beyond politically motivated disinformation, many otherwise well-intentioned commentaries unknowingly spread false or misleading narratives, muddling or ignoring the intentional ambiguity baked into the U.S. and its major allies' official positions. For example, in September 2022 the U.S.' most prestigious, highly viewed nonpartisan news magazine show – *60 Minutes* – erroneously told over ten million live broadcast viewers that "US policy since 1979 has been to recognize Taiwan as part of China." Many millions more around the world were subsequently exposed to this misleading claim after the clip seeded global headlines for containing a statement from Biden widely interpreted to constitute a pledge to defend Taiwan if China attacks (CBS News 2022). In recent years, many analysts seem just as likely to falsely equate U.S. allies' official positions on Taiwan's status with Beijing's "one-China principle" as to reiterate poorly substantiated assertions that key allies are radically transforming their positions and policies vis-à-vis Taiwan. For example, since 2021 numerous commentaries have falsely asserted that famously cautious and constitutionally constrained Japan is now more explicitly committed Taiwan's defense than even the United States itself (Liff 2022a).

In short, with unprecedented global attention on Taiwan and the Taiwan Strait, the noise:signal ratio about U.S. allies' diverse approaches – past and present – is unsettlingly high. As U.S. leaders assert solidarity among allies and concerns about the Taiwan Strait have surged to the point that the 2023 G7 summit statement "call[s] for a peaceful resolution of cross-Strait issues" and (vaguely) asserts that "There is no change in the basic positions of the G7 members on Taiwan, including stated one China policies" (G7 2023b), greater clarity on what key allies' positions and policies actually are is essential. Careful historical baselines and a well-considered analytical framework with which to assess recent developments across numerous cases are also needed.

In an earlier, more halcyon era of increasing cooperation and engagement both across the Strait and between Beijing and Washington, an insular focus on the U.S.-PRC-Taiwan triangle was understandable, though still problematic. Given highly volatile contemporary realities, however, it is increasingly ill-advised. Though the agency of and decisions by Beijing and Taipei are of course fundamental, and beyond the Strait Washington has a singularly important role to play, the agency and significance of U.S. allies have for too long been excessively discounted or ignored altogether. U.S. allies' choices have always been, and will remain, important variables affecting Taiwan's international space, peace and stability across the Taiwan Strait, and the course a conflict could take if deterrence fails.

1.5 Bringing U.S. Allies Back In

This Element surveys the respective origins and evolutions of the positions, effective policies, and stated interests concerning Taiwan and the Taiwan Strait of six major democratic U.S. treaty allies and the European Union. It also briefly highlights a foundational contribution from a seventh ally – Canada – and several recent related developments concerning the North Atlantic Treaty Organization (NATO), of which the United States, Canada, and other key European treaty allies are founding members. This study's extensive empirical survey contributes to academic literatures and policy debates by highlighting the consequential but oft-overlooked roles played by U.S. allies past, present, and potentially future. Furthermore, its original comparative analysis sheds light on key issues impossible to descry from single case-centric approaches. Two contributions are particularly noteworthy:

1.5.1 Highlighting U.S. Allies' Agency, Trailblazing, and Significance Historically and Today

Much of the decades-old U.S.-centric academic and policy-oriented literatures regarding Taiwan- and Taiwan Strait-related issues has treated the agency, positions, and policies of key U.S. allies as an afterthought, if not neglecting them entirely. This oversight matters for two primary reasons: First, Beijing's increasingly coercive posture vis-à-vis Taipei and a rapidly changing balance of power today all but guarantee that several major U.S. treaty allies (e.g., Japan) and economic partners (e.g., the EU) are and will continue to be essential partners for Taipei and Washington in achieving core strategic and policy objectives. Accordingly, understanding where these governments stand on key issues, as well as what they have been willing to do and say over time in support of Taiwan and the cross-Strait status quo, has real-world implications for policy.

Second, overlooking the agency and significance of U.S. allies is also profoundly ahistorical. Contrary to the widespread impression today that the U.S. has always been in the lead, with allies grudgingly following (or not), throughout the post-1949 period Western Pacific and European allies made significant contributions to enabling Taiwan's international space and cross-Strait peace and stability even as they sought to develop ties with the much larger PRC. Importantly, they have done so variably in concert with and independently from the United States – at times even over Washington's direct opposition. At critical historical moments now often forgotten, allies' political leaders effectively blazed trails that the U.S. would later follow.

Not only did most major U.S. democratic treaty allies switch official diplomatic recognition from the ROC to the PRC many years before Washington did.

As the case studies in Sections 2–4 demonstrate, it was also a major U.S. ally – not the U.S. government – that first implemented each of several measures designed to square the difficult circle of establishing diplomatic relations with Beijing while supporting continued engagement with Taiwan and cross-Strait peace and stability. Of particular note: it was a U.S. ally that first (1) recognized the PRC government without endorsing Beijing's sovereignty claim over Taiwan and (2) negotiated a bilateral communique with Beijing that avoided any mention of Taiwan. And it was also a U.S. ally that, even after switching official diplomatic recognition from the ROC to the PRC, first (3) linked recognition of Beijing to "peaceful resolution" of the cross-Strait dispute; (4) implemented the "do not endorse, do not challenge" framework that later became the heart of the U.S. position on "One China"; (5) insisted on a de facto representative office in Taipei; (6) initiated robust engagement with KMT leaders through legislative exchanges that functioned as stand-ins for direct high-level government-to-government engagement; (7); sent a cabinet-level official to Taipei; (8) allowed a visit by a sitting ROC foreign minister.

1.5.2 Highlighting the Politically Contingent Variability of Allies' Effective Taiwan Policies

This study also adopts a unique comparative approach. It reveals important variation across and within cases concerning how political leaders have chosen to operationalize "unofficial" relations with Taiwan, including how to speak publicly about or act in support of Taiwan's international space or cross-Strait peace and stability. This analysis helps reveal the under-appreciated ambiguity, dynamism, and political contingency at the heart of the "One China" framework that for decades has shaped the contours of the U.S. and many of its allies' approaches. Short of a widely understood red-line – official recognition of the ROC/Taiwan as a sovereign state – the empirical record across these cases reveals that a country's "One China policy" is, as far as official rhetoric regarding and practical engagement with Taiwan is concerned, largely whatever government leaders choose to make of it.

The diversity of effective Taiwan policies even among the United States and its closest democratic treaty allies revealed by this comparative approach throws into sharp relief the strikingly weak correlation between a government's abstract, usually static, official position on "One China" (form) and its effective official policies and rhetoric regarding Taiwan and the Taiwan Strait (substance). In any practical sense, even after recognizing Beijing major allies' effective policies on Taiwan-related matters have varied widely, with significant real-world implications for Taiwan's international space and cross-Strait vicissitudes.

Importantly, this variation manifests both across and within the cases examined in this Element. Regarding the former, even ally and partner governments adopting identical – or nearly identical – official positions on "One China" have engaged in widely divergent conduct in terms of bilateral engagement with or public expressions of support for Taiwan and/or cross-Strait peace and stability. Concerning the latter, despite the general contemporary trends among major U.S. democratic allies and partners toward closer unofficial ties with Taipei and greater outspokenness regarding Taiwan's international space and the Taiwan Strait, history suggests that these trends are not inevitably linear or unidirectional. Several case studies reveal that shifting domestic and international political winds have intermittently caused some political leaders to reevaluate the pros and cons of more robust engagement with and outspokenness concerning Taipei, and to adjust their approaches accordingly.

In aggregate, the case studies introduced in Sections 2–4 highlight the underappreciated and immense historical significance of U.S. allies' positions and policies vis-a-vis Taiwan: for Taiwan itself, for cross-Strait dynamics, and even for the U.S.' own positions and policies. They also highlight their practically consequential variability – across and within cases.

1.6 A New Era for U.S. Allies and the Taiwan Strait?

Concomitant with the worsening of relations between Beijing and Taipei, as well as between China and the United States and many of its allies, recent years have witnessed unprecedented multilateralization and internationalization of concerns about "peace and stability across the Taiwan Strait," calls for "peaceful resolution of cross-Strait issues," and support for Taiwan's democracy and "meaningful participation" in the international community.

This contemporary trend manifests in manifold ways. Most conspicuous is the recent proliferation of official rhetoric appearing in high-level unilateral, bilateral, and multilateral statements from U.S. allied governments, resolutions passed by national parliaments, and exchanges of legislators. Several allies show newfound (or rediscovered) willingness to conduct naval transits through the international waters of the Taiwan Strait, and/or quietly share dual-use (military + civilian) and other technologies with Taiwan. Meanwhile, especially since 2022 witnessed Russia's full-scale invasion of Ukraine and the PLA's massive exercises around Taiwan, various indicators suggest a sharp uptick in discussions among the U.S. and its allies about military and/or economic contingency plans in the event of a cross-Strait crisis.

Recent developments also demonstrate that many U.S. allies increasingly recognize their own national interests and agency in cross-Strait peace and stability. Regardless of each government's ability to project substantial military power to the area surrounding Taiwan – extremely limited in most cases outside the Western Pacific – their economic and financial tools are highly salient. Not only do the United States and its democratic treaty allies account for eight of the world's ten largest economies (China and democratic India round out the list), four of Beijing's top five trading partners in 2022 were the EU (#1), of which the largest national economies are all U.S. treaty allies; Japan (#3); South Korea (#4); and Germany (#5). The other (#2) is the United States itself (Haiguan Zongshu 2023). Accordingly, the potential to shape Beijing's behavior of even distant U.S. European allies, and the EU itself, should not be dismissed. Even in the military domain, U.S. NATO allies could make a significant indirect contribution in peacetime or a crisis by adjusting their deployments and mission sets to make it easier for the U.S. military to prioritize the Western Pacific. In short, U.S. allies possess substantial potential capability and leverage, regardless of geography.

1.7 Overview of the Element

This Element aims to introduce readers to key issues related to U.S. allies and the Taiwan Strait, and to do so in a manner widely accessible for scholars, policymakers, students, and the public.

Section 2 gives readers a crash course in the basic history of the post-1949 disputes over "One China" and Taiwan's status at the heart of contemporary cross-Strait frictions. It highlights the critically important but widely misunderstood distinction between Beijing's self-defined "one-China *principle*," which asserts that Taiwan belongs to the PRC, and the U.S. and other major allies' "One China" *policies*, which today generally neither endorse nor challenge the PRC's sovereignty claim. Highlighting Canada's innovative 1970 framework and using the famously consequential case of U.S. Taiwan policy after 1979 as an illustrative example, this section also introduces the study's basic analytical framework. This framework aims to elucidate not only allied governments' abstract official positions on Taiwan's status but also how their political leaders have sought to operationalize that position in practical terms: that is, through their effective policies and rhetoric vis-à-vis Taiwan and the Taiwan Strait.

Sections 3 and 4 apply the aforementioned analytical framework to an original empirical survey of the post-1949 histories and evolution of six major democratic U.S. treaty allies' positions, perspectives, and policies vis-à-vis Taiwan/the Taiwan Strait. These case studies focus on the U.S.' most wealthy, economically advanced and militarily capable allies in the Western Pacific and Western Europe. Not coincidentally, these are also the half-dozen U.S. allies who trade the most with China. Listed in chronological order of each government's decision to recognize the PRC, the former cases are Japan (1972), Australia (1972), and South Korea (1992). The latter cases are the United Kingdom (1950)[1], France (1964), and Germany (1972). Section 4 additionally examines two important, but unique, non-nation-state cases: the EU (1975) and NATO.

Collectively, these case studies demonstrate the diversity and variability of U.S. allies' approaches to Taiwan, past and present. They reveal their significant historical agency, as well as the extent to which Beijing's increasingly coercive posture and assertion of its preferred narrative on "One China" today are generating an unprecedented international reaction and alignment of allied rhetoric and policy, even in far-off Europe, the long-term implications of which remain to be seen.

Each ally/partner case study first introduces the government's foundational position on "One China" – including on the critical question of whether upon recognizing the PRC the government endorsed Beijing's claim of sovereignty over Taiwan.[2] It then briefly summarizes post-normalization approaches to Taiwan and the Taiwan Strait, with a particular focus on (a) the extent and nature of engagement with Taiwan and support for its international space and (b) official statements and policies as it relates to cross-Strait frictions.

These eight brief case studies aim to cut through the U.S.-centrism and abstract and often misleading talk of "principle" that permeates the discourse. Instead, they highlight the practical reality of significant variability and dynamism in major democratic U.S. treaty allies' policies toward Taiwan both across cases and within them (i.e., over time). Collectively, they demonstrate that a government's effective Taiwan policy can be, but is not necessarily, dynamic – even if its official decades-old position on "One China" is frozen in time. It can shift subtly and/or significantly in response to the vagaries of PRC policies toward Taiwan or its leaders' evolving assessments of national interests and domestic and international political dynamics.

Sections 5 and 6 summarize major takeaways. In aggregate, this study's findings challenge conventional understandings of a key issue in East Asian international relations. Although Washington has always been and is almost certain to remain both Taiwan's most important international partner and the primary external player in cross-Strait deterrence, major democratic U.S. allies (and the EU) have long had, and continue to have, major roles to play. Looking ahead, a rapidly changing balance of power and influence ensures that

---

[1] As noted in Section 4, the UK and China did not achieve ambassador-level exchanges until 1972.
[2] As explained more fully in Section 4, as an alliance organization – not a government – NATO is unique among these cases in not having a position on "One China."

U.S. allies' policy choices will remain crucial variables affecting Taiwan's and U.S. policy options in both peacetime and a potential crisis.

Recent developments make clear that today, arguably for the first time, peace and stability across the Taiwan Strait are widely considered a common challenge for the United States and its major democratic treaty allies in the Western Pacific and Europe. As such, it is critically important that scholars, policymakers, students, and citizens better understand the past and present evolution of U.S. allies' intentionally nuanced positions and policies vis-à-vis Taiwan and the "One China" question.

2 "One China" and the Taiwan Strait: The Distinction between Beijing's "Principle" and the U.S. and Allies' "Policies"

> In the United States' relations with both China and Taiwan, the verbal formulations used to describe policy are more important than perhaps in any other foreign policy relationship. Indeed, words themselves become policy.
> –Former AIT Chairman Richard Bush (2017, 3)

The ostensible trigger for the PLA's unprecedentedly large-scale August 2022 military exercises – a long-postponed and mostly symbolic visit to Taipei by outgoing U.S. Speaker of the House Nancy Pelosi – was revealing on multiple levels. As important as the advanced military capabilities Beijing demonstrated were the assumptions outside the PRC that gave the crisis its meaning internationally: above all, that many believed Beijing might risk a catastrophic war over its claim to Taiwan.

As told by Beijing, the PRC's furious response was due to Pelosi's alleged violation of past U.S. commitments to its "one-China principle." As detailed below, an essential component of this "principle" – *as Beijing defines it* – is that self-governed, democratic Taiwan, which the PRC has never ruled, belongs to it. Accordingly, China's Ministry of Foreign Affairs (MFA) called Pelosi's visit to "*China's Taiwan region* . . . a serious violation of the one-China principle and . . . a seriously wrong signal to the separatist forces for 'Taiwan independence'" [emphasis added]. Beijing further asserted its unilateral interpretation of U.S. policy, stating that "Congress, as a part of the U.S. Government, is inherently obliged to strictly observe the one-China policy of the U.S. Government and refrain from having any official exchanges" (MFA(PRC) 2022). Beijing frequently makes similar claims about U.S. allies. For example, following each of a series of recent visits to Taipei by German parliamentarians, the PRC Embassy in Berlin asserted: "The German side is not allowed to have any official contacts with Taiwan, and that also applies to German parliamentarians. This principle is part of the One China policy" (e.g., *Anadolu Agency* 2023).

Beijing has for decades also claimed that the U.S. and all other foreign governments having diplomatic relations with the PRC "recognize that there is only one China and that the government of the People's Republic of China is the sole legal government of China and Taiwan is part of China" (State Council 1993). Today, it frequently asserts that a "universal consensus" exists in the international community in support of Beijing's "one-China principle" (MFA(PRC) 2020).

Yet, such claims are best understood as self-interested and misleading propaganda, not historical fact. For starters, no leader in Taiwan endorses Beijing's claim that Taiwan is PRC territory. Nor do the dozen foreign governments that still recognize the ROC as a sovereign state. Most importantly for this study, and notwithstanding Beijing's unilateral assertions to the contrary, Washington and its major democratic treaty allies did not endorse Beijing's claim of sovereignty over Taiwan upon recognizing the PRC.

Today, as China's frictions with the United States and its major democratic allies worsen and Beijing more brazenly tries to define for them what their "One China" policies are, both Taiwan's status and the very "rules" governing the "One China" framework's operation in international politics are becoming increasingly contested, and publicly so (Liff and Lin 2022). Rare public pushback from the German Foreign Office in 2022 against Beijing's repeated misrepresentations of German policy was one remarkable demonstration that the distinction between the PRC's "principle" and other foreign governments' policies is not a matter only for U.S.-China relations. Rather, it is also fundamental to major U.S. allies' approaches. In strikingly candid prepared remarks, a senior German Foreign Office official stated, "We steadfastly reject [Beijing's term "one-China principle"] and the notion behind that. [*sic*] We have our One China policy ... But, it is us who have devised this policy and it is us who interpret this policy – no one else" (Thümmel 2022).

This section has two primary goals: (1) to concisely summarize for readers the history of the "one-China principle," its international contestation, and the broad contours of U.S. Taiwan policy, and (2) to introduce the study's analytical framework that the latter inspires. In service of these objectives, the remainder of this section is divided into four sections: The first section summarizes the "One China" idea as it has manifested across the Taiwan Strait since Chiang Kai-shek and his Nationalist Party (KMT) in 1949 fled the mainland for Taiwan after their defeat in the Chinese Civil War. The next section introduces the concept of the "One China" framework and its significance in international politics. The penultimate section reviews key pillars of the U.S.' famously ambiguous "One China" policy to highlight for the reader two major points: First, the U.S.' position regarding Taiwan's status is fundamentally distinct from Beijing's "one-China principle," which the U.S. government does not endorse. Second, this ambiguity has granted U.S. political leaders considerable latitude to support both cross-Strait stability and "robust unofficial relations" with Taiwan – despite the absence of official diplomatic relations with Taipei since 1979. Using the best-known U.S. case as inspiration, the section closes by introducing the two-step analytical framework employed in the allied case studies in Sections 3 and 4.

2.1 The "One-China Principle(s)" and the Post-1949 Cross-Strait Dispute

Scholars have long considered the question of how to settle Taiwan's ambiguous international status the most fundamental question in China's foreign and security policy. China's leaders agree. For instance, the PRC's ambassador to the UK repeated a common refrain when he warned in August 2022 that Beijing's "one-China principle" is the "political foundation for the development of relations between China and all countries in the world" (*The Guardian* 2022a). As this statement makes clear, the issue is not merely of concern to the governments on both sides of the Taiwan Strait. Rather, it has been a defining issue in both the PRC's and Republic of China's (ROC) foreign relations since 1949 – especially in dealings with the United States and its major democratic treaty allies.

The 1949 CCP victory in the Chinese civil war led to three major outcomes most relevant to this study. First, Mao Zedong declared the establishment in Beijing of a new CCP-led People's Republic that believed itself to have "replaced the previous KMT regime" as the sole legal successor state of the ROC and "the only legitimate government of the whole of China," including Taiwan (State Council 2022). Second, after fleeing to Taiwan, Chiang proclaimed Taipei the ROC's new "provisional" capital, while simultaneously declaring his intent to eventually reestablish ROC control over the mainland. Third, the KMT's authoritarian government denied the Taiwan-born majority living in Taiwan at the time a chance at self-determination. From 1949 until the 1980s, the period during which the United States and most major allies formalized their official positions on "One China," the KMT used its fear of a communist insurgency and claim to be the government of *all* of China to justify martial law and at times brutal oppression in Taiwan.

In short, after 1949 the cross-Strait status quo was effectively frozen, with a KMT-led ROC government in Taipei and a CCP-led PRC government in Beijing. Each side considered the other illegitimate and vowed to "reunify" Taiwan and the mainland under their party's control. The net result was single-party authoritarian governments on both sides of the Taiwan Strait – both run by

U.S. Allies and the Taiwan Strait 15

elites born on the mainland and both making mutually irreconcilable claims to be the sole legitimate government of a China that included the mainland and Taiwan.

2.1.1 Origins and Cold War Manifestations of "One China" across the Taiwan Strait

Although some historical records suggest that key CCP and KMT leaders did not even consider Taiwan part of China before the 1940s, by 1949 the political meaning and significance of Taiwan for both sides had fundamentally changed. The idea that Taiwan was "inherent Chinese territory" had become nonnegotiable (Hsiao and Sullivan 1979; Wachman 2007, chaps. 4–5).

The concept of "One China" originated internationally in opposition to two alternatives for resolving the post-1949 cross-Strait dispute, both anathema to PRC and ROC leaders during the Cold War: "two Chinas" (*liang ge Zhongguo*), which envisioned the international community recognizing the legitimacy of both the PRC and ROC, and "one China, one Taiwan" (*yi Zhong yi Tai*), which envisioned the international community recognizing Taiwan as an independent state disconnected from both the PRC or ROC regimes.

In theory, Taiwan's legal status could have been resolved after 1945 during the negotiations over a peace treaty with Japan – Taiwan's colonial occupier from 1895 to 1945. However, different views among the allies concerning which to invite meant neither the PRC nor the ROC government was represented at the 1951 San Francisco Conference. The text of the resulting treaty stated only that "Japan renounces all right, title and claim to Formosa and the Pescadores." Critically, it said nothing about to which entity sovereignty over them was subsequently transferred ("Treaty of Peace with Japan" 1951). Nor was this ambiguity explicitly resolved in Japan's subsequent peace treaties with the ROC ("Treaty of Peace"1952) and PRC ("Treaty of Peace and Friendship" 1978).

After North Korea's (PRC-supported) invasion of South Korea in June 1950 threw into sharp relief the risk of a hot war of unification in East Asia, U.S. President Truman stated that Taiwan was not yet part of China and should be considered an issue of continuing international concern, and that the people on Taiwan should have some say in their future. The U.S. continued to recognize the ROC government – a UN founding member state – but, importantly, did not recognize its "ownership of the island" (Bush 2004, 95). Generally speaking, the United States, the UK, and other key U.S. allies either judged that Taiwan's status remained "undetermined" or avoided publicly taking any explicit legal position on Taiwan's relationship to the PRC. Unsurprisingly, both the PRC and

ROC governments took issue with these positions, instead claiming sovereignty over Taiwan for themselves.

Although in policy discourse today the "one-China principle" is generally associated with the PRC's claim of sovereignty over Taiwan, to understand how the contemporary status quo came to be one must not forget that throughout the Cold War the ROC government in Taipei also enforced its own version of the "one-China principle." In the view of Chiang's KMT, it was the ROC, not the PRC, that was the sole legitimate government of a single "China" including both Taiwan and the mainland.

Given the two sides' irreconcilable "one-China principles," throughout the Cold War all foreign governments had to make a choice: recognize *either* the PRC *or* the ROC as China's sole legal government. Accordingly, and of profound historical and contemporary significance, both Beijing *and* Taipei repeatedly rejected efforts before 1971 by the United States, the UK, Japan, Canada, and other foreign governments to explore possibilities for a "two Chinas" or a "one China, one Taiwan" solution. As Bush points out, the world will never know whether, if the KMT had been more receptive to the U.S. and others' efforts to facilitate dual presence in the UN for both the PRC and ROC, Taiwan "might still be represented in international organizations today" (2004, 120).

Two major turning points in the history of the "one-China principle" were particularly consequential internationally. The first – in the 1970s – witnessed a cascade of foreign governments switching official recognition from the ROC to the PRC. Two major catalysts were U.S. President Richard Nixon's surprise July 1971 announcement of his intent to visit the PRC, which signaled a historic rapprochement between Washington and Beijing, and, three months later, a resolution granting PRC representatives seats in the UN Security Council and General Assembly and expelling "the representatives of Chiang Kai-shek." Between 1970 and 1973, dozens of foreign governments recognized the PRC, including U.S. allies Canada, Italy, Japan, (West) Germany, Australia, and New Zealand. (The UK, which had recognized the PRC in 1950 but not yet established full diplomatic relations, also exchanged ambassadors with Beijing for the first time.) The consequences for the ROC's international recognition were profound: in accordance with the two sides' irreconcilable "one-China principles," all these foreign governments either severed, or saw Taipei sever, diplomatic relations.

2.1.2 Taiwan's Democratization and Its Impact

The second major turning point occurred in the late 1980s and 1990s, a period which witnessed both the Cold War's end (1989–1991) and Taiwan's rapid democratization after four decades of martial law and single-party KMT rule.

Democratization gave the long-oppressed Taiwan-born majority a central role in Taiwan's politics, including greater influence over Taiwan's complicated relationships with both the mainland and the "One China" concept itself. The consequences for cross-Strait relations were profound.

The first breakthrough occurred under KMT President Lee Teng-hui (1988–2000) – the ROC's first Taiwan-born, first post-martial law, and, after 1996, first democratically elected leader. In 1991, the ROC government declared the end of the Period of Mobilization against Communist Rebellion, effectively ending the Chinese civil war from Taipei's perspective and identifying the PRC as an "equal political entity" with which it could engage. It also recognized that the government in Taipei effectively controls only the islands of Taiwan, Penghu, Kinmen, and Matsu, while the PRC government exercises authority over mainland China (Chen 2022, 1031–32; Somers 2023, 693). This facilitated cross-Strait contacts and economic linkages, as well as massive investment from Taiwan into the mainland. Later, as a clear indication of generational change and increasingly open political contestation within rapidly democratizing Taiwan regarding "One China," in 1999 Lee publicly referred to Taiwan and the mainland as having "special state-to-state relations." His successor, Taiwan's first DPP president, Chen Shui-bian (2000–2008), took such rhetoric even further. Chen, who was also Taiwan-born, referred to "one country on each side" (of the Strait) (Chen 2022, 1033). He even pursued a controversial referendum on Taiwan's UN membership. Such moves, widely seen as flirting with a unilateral declaration of de jure independence – a potential casus belli for Beijing – generated significant blowback, including from the United States and key allies. Based in part on this experience, Taiwan's second DPP president, Tsai Ing-wen (2016–2024), adopted a more moderate, status quo–oriented stance. Her successor, William Lai (2024–), says that he plans to follow suit.

Beyond the consequences for cross-Strait relations, the implications of Taiwan's democratization for more flexible engagement with foreign governments were also significant. The era of Taipei's rigid assertion of the KMT's version of the "one-China principle" internationally was effectively over. In 1989, the ROC for the first time allowed a foreign government (Grenada) to normalize diplomatic relations without requiring it to sever diplomatic ties with the PRC (Mengin 1997, 240).

Thus, when reflecting on the origins of the U.S. and its allies' decades-old positions on "One China," one should not forget that throughout the Cold War both the PRC and ROC governments actively enforced their respective positions that Taiwan is part of one "China." Both considered any proposal to treat it as anything but unacceptable, thereby forcing a choice on all foreign governments. In contrast, today, only the PRC actively enforces a version – its version – of the "one-China principle" internationally. Though differences today between Taiwan's major political parties on cross-Strait issues are significant, none accepts Beijing's contention that the ROC/Taiwan is part of, or subordinate to, the CCP-led PRC (see Table 1).

Although under KMT President Ma Ying-jeou (2008–2016) Taiwan significantly deepened cooperation with Beijing based on the KMT's and CCP's shared conviction that there is only one "China" and Taiwan belongs to that "China," the fundamental disagreement between the two parties regarding to *which* "China" (ROC vs. PRC) Taiwan belongs persists. Whereas the KMT openly acknowledges this reality based on the formula of "one country, respective interpretations," the PRC does not (Chen 2022, 1034–35; Somers 2023, 695–96). As noted earlier and summarized in Table 1, the party of Ma's DPP successors has a very different view, even as both Presidents Tsai and Lai have adopted a moderate stance in office.

Beyond the Strait, one major consequence of Taiwan's democratization and its leaders' post–Cold War shifts toward greater flexibility and pragmatism on "One China" was to further expand space for the U.S. and its democratic treaty allies to, in the words of Klintworth, "stretch the principle of one China into the reality of a one China, one Taiwan policy" (1993, 87–90). The past three decades have witnessed deepening economic and other ties across the Taiwan

Table 1 Major party positions on "One China," Taiwan's sovereignty, and China's international representation (Chen 2022, 1038)

	CCP	KMT	DPP
"One China"	There is only one China in the world.	There is only one China in the world.	Taiwan should renounce the claim of "One China."
Taiwan's sovereignty	Taiwan is part of "China" – the PRC.	Taiwan is part of "China" – the ROC.	Taiwan is already a sovereign state under the name of the ROC.
China's representation	The PRC is the legitimate, exclusive representative of China.	"One country, respective interpretations" (OCRI)	Taiwan should not seek to represent "China."

Strait, an increasingly robust "Taiwanese" identity within Taiwan, and a major expansion of foreign governments' "unofficial" engagement with Taipei. Even so, support for the "status quo" remains widespread (Election Study Center 2024).

2.2 The Contested "One China" Framework Internationally: Intentionally Ambiguous and Politically Contingent

Upon recognizing the PRC as the "sole legal government of China," neither the United States nor any major democratic U.S. ally endorsed Beijing's claim of sovereignty over Taiwan. In the decades since, each country's leaders have made a series of political decisions about how to operationalize their intentionally vague position on the sovereignty question in terms of concrete policies and bilateral engagement with Taipei and on cross-Strait issues. Not based upon any explicit commitment to Beijing, the effective bounds of "appropriate" policies have always been conditioned on international and domestic political vicissitudes, interpreted through political leaders' complex and evolving calculus of national interest, including the risks of instability.

The events of August 2022 are a case in point. PRC disinformation to the contrary, under its "One China" policy the United States does not commit to "prevent" a sitting Speaker of the house from visiting Taiwan. In fact, Pelosi's trip was not even the first by a sitting Speaker. Even so, President Biden reportedly discouraged her from making the trip based on the Pentagon's judgment that "it's not a good idea." Pelosi herself even suggested Beijing might shoot her plane down (*UPI* 2022). Biden's alleged effort to discourage Pelosi's visit is an extremely high-profile example of how concerns about Beijing's reactions – or anticipated reactions – to bilateral engagements with or rhetoric/policies in support of Taiwan often lead to political judgments that are, in effect, self-imposed restrictions. Where the "line" exists is difficult to judge and politically contingent.

2.2.1 The "One China Framework"

Informing this Element's analytical approach is the idea that the "One China" framework functions in international politics as something akin to what political scientists call an "informal institution" (Liff and Lin 2022). Put simply, U.S. allies' effective policies toward Taiwan and the Taiwan Strait are contingent on leaders' interpretations of largely unwritten, socially constructed, and domestically and internationally contested rules that shape "many of the 'real' incentives and constraints that underlie [leaders'] political behaviour" (Helmke and Levitsky 2003). Short of the widely understood red line of formal recognition of the ROC/Taiwan as a sovereign state, U.S. allies' respective "One China" policies are largely what their leaders choose to make them. The caveat, of course, is that certain actions have consequences, and certain moves may elicit Beijing's wrath. But where even that line is, or how likely Beijing is to back up its often fiery rhetoric with costly punishment, is often unclear.

Far from being based on any legally binding, clearly articulated, or explicit commitment to Beijing, it is subjective and politically conditioned interpretations of what "One China" means in principle and practice – and what their government's interests are – that determine how political leaders choose to operationalize their respective positions in terms of actual policies vis-à-vis Taiwan. Judgments about where the "appropriate" or "acceptable" bounds on engagement with Taiwan and on cross-Strait issues lie and what policies best serve national interests effectively define the "rules of the game." Political leaders must decide how proactive (or passive) their respective Taiwan policies should be, and in which domains – economic, cultural, political, military, etc. – they can or should engage Taipei.

No case better illustrates the flexible, politically conditioned bounds of a foreign government's "One China" policy than that of the United States, Taiwan's closest international partner and the ROC's erstwhile treaty ally.

2.3 The Most Famous Case in Point: U.S. "One China" Policy 101

Frequent disinformation and misinformation in contemporary discourse to the contrary, the difference between Beijing's self-defined "one-China principle" and the U.S. "One China" policy is well-established. In the U.S. case, the term "One China policy" is best understood as encapsulating not only the U.S. official position on "One China" (read: Taiwan's status), but also how the U.S. engages Taiwan sans official diplomatic ties and in support of Washington's long-standing position that cross-Strait differences should be resolved peacefully (Bush 2017, 18).

Although in the interest of stable relations the U.S. government generally avoids highlighting the distinction between its position and Beijing's "one-China principle" publicly, there are exceptions – typically in response to PRC disinformation campaigns. In a 2020 speech, for example, Trump administration Assistant Secretary of State David Stilwell criticized Beijing for "distorting" history. He noted that the U.S. "one-China policy ... is distinct from Beijing's 'One China principle' under which the Chinese Communist Party asserts sovereignty over Taiwan," adding that "The U.S. takes no position on sovereignty over Taiwan" (Stilwell 2020). Following another round of disinformation from Beijing after Pelosi's 2022 visit, Biden's State Department released the following statement: "The PRC continues to publicly misrepresent U.S. policy. The United States does not subscribe to the PRC's "one China principle" – we remain committed to our long-standing, bipartisan one China policy, guided by the Taiwan Relations Act, Three Joint Communiques, and Six Assurances" (@StateDeptSpox 2022).

As this response demonstrates, the U.S. "One China" policy is not defined in a single document or any bilateral agreement or treaty with Beijing. Rather, it is the effective culmination of decades of unilateral statements, modified contact guidelines, three bilateral communiques with Beijing, domestic legislation such as the 1979 Taiwan Relations Act, presidential decisions such as the recently declassified 1982 *Six Assurances*, and various policies developed and implemented long after the United States officially switched diplomatic recognition from Taipei to Beijing in 1979 (CRS 2015). Far from being static, beyond the abstract question of "One China," in any practical sense U.S. Taiwan policy has evolved significantly since the 1970s. Indeed, as Bush (2004, 121) noted twenty years ago, "U.S. relations with Taiwan today are far more robust in substance than they are in form ... Washington has richer ties with Taipei on an unofficial basis than it does with many countries with which it has diplomatic relations." Bush's point is even more compelling today.

An extensive academic literature on U.S. Taiwan policy already exists. So, too, do manifold government documents describing U.S. policy and strategic objectives vis-à-vis Taiwan (American Institute in Taiwan 2022). Accordingly, the following summary serves only to highlight for unfamiliar readers key features of U.S. Taiwan policy and to clarify the basis for the analytical framework applied in Sections 3 and 4 to the lesser-known cases of major U.S. treaty allies.

Of fundamental importance is the following: Upon normalizing relations with Beijing in 1979, the U.S. government recognized the PRC as China's "sole legal government." Critically, however, Washington never endorsed the second essential element of Beijing's "one-China principle": its claim that Taiwan is part of the PRC. Instead, in the 1979 communique the U.S. government merely "acknowledges *the Chinese position* that there is but one China and Taiwan is part of China" [emphasis added] (AIT 1979).

In adopting this intentionally ambiguous position, the U.S. embraced a version of the 1970 "Canadian formula." The rationale for this formula warrants a brief aside, especially because (1) it is the most direct inspiration for the U.S. and many other governments' official positions on "One China," and (2) the basic "acknowledge but do not recognize" framework in the 1972 and 1979 U.S.-PRC communiques is widely – but wrongly – considered a U.S. invention.

2.3.1 The "Canadian Formula" (1970)

After becoming prime minister in 1968, Pierre Trudeau launched normalization negotiations with Beijing – over Washington's opposition. Consistent with Ottawa's 1950s-era position that Taiwan's status remained "an undetermined international issue," however, Canadian diplomats were tasked by Trudeau with "avoid[ing] any commitment that would deny Canada the possibility of recognizing Taiwan as an independent state at some time in the future if circumstances should make that feasible" (Cabinet 1969; Simon 2023, 4). Though initially hoping to avoid severing official ties with Taipei altogether, Canada eventually agreed to end de jure recognition of the ROC government. Even so, Canadian negotiators repeatedly rejected Beijing's demands to recognize the PRC's sovereignty claim (Frolic 2022, Ch. 2).

In the landmark October 1970 Canada–PRC normalization communique, Ottawa "recognizes" the PRC "as the sole legal government of China" but merely "takes note of" Beijing's position on Taiwan. As Mitchell Sharp, then Canada's foreign secretary, explained to the House of Commons, Ottawa intentionally neither "endorsed" nor "challenged" the PRC's position. Sharp's contemporaneous exchanges with opposition party leaders elucidate both how the ROC government's insistence that it represented "all" of China tied Ottawa's hands and that, despite that fact, Canada still did not endorse Beijing's sovereignty claim. Asked whether recognition of the PRC meant Ottawa would break off relations with "the government of Taiwan," Sharp replied, matter-of-factly, that "there is no government of Taiwan." He added that Ottawa and Taipei agreed that it is "not possible to recognize simultaneously more than one government as the government of China." A comment from the New Democratic Party's leader drove home the broad political support for Canada's non-endorsement of Beijing's "one-China principle." After volunteering that he was "very glad" to support Canada's diplomatic relations with "mainland China," he added that "when the government of Taiwan is prepared to state that it is the government of that area, and of that area only, it will be time for the Canadian government to negotiate with that government for diplomatic recognition" (House of Commons (Canada) 1970, 49–51).

Thus, in 1970 Canada became the first democratic U.S. ally to mention "Taiwan" explicitly in a normalization communique – a condition imposed by Beijing to avoid a repeat of what happened with France in 1964 (see Section 4). Even so, even the fairly China-friendly Trudeau government refused to endorse Beijing's sovereignty claim. Thenceforth, the "Canadian Formula" would become the basis for the U.S. and other democratic allies' future, similarly ambiguous, positions on "One China." The long-term consequences for Taiwan's international space and the cross-Strait status quo were profound.

2.3.2 The 1979 U.S. Position

The U.S. government's limited acknowledgment (and non-endorsement) of the PRC position in its own normalization communique with Beijing nearly nine years after Canada's amounted to a political (but not legal) commitment not to actively support a "One China, One Taiwan" or "Two Chinas" framework, or a declaration by Taiwan of de jure independence. Importantly, however, the U.S. formula neither endorsed as a goal nor ruled out the possibilities of either (1) eventual unification with the mainland or (2) independence for and U.S. recognition of Taiwan as a sovereign state. It is a policy statement implying that Washington is officially neutral on the negotiated outcome, provided it is reached peacefully by the two sides (Romberg 2003, 35).

Accordingly, core pillars of U.S. policy were (and remain) opposition to the use of force and any unilateral change to the status quo – by either side. In 1982, the Reagan administration reaffirmed that "the United States government takes no position on Taiwan's sovereignty. We regard this as a matter to be determined by the Chinese people on both sides of the Strait" (Bush 2004, 121). More than forty years later, at a November 2023 meeting, Biden reportedly conveyed a similar message directly to Xi Jinping, noting, "We do not take a position on the ultimate resolution of cross-Strait differences, provided they are resolved peacefully" (Lawrence 2024). In short, and as noted later, U.S. administrations of both parties have long considered Taiwan's current status undetermined and take no position on what its future status should be.

2.3.3 The U.S.' Effective Taiwan Policy: Substance over Form

In candid moments, even high-ranking U.S. officials such as Biden's National Security Advisor Jake Sullivan admit that U.S. Taiwan policy is "not a model of clarity" and is "built on a series of internal tensions." Yet the U.S. government's vague position is by design. It has in practice enabled significant policy flexibility in support of what Sullivan defines as the long-standing "practical objective" of U.S. "One China" policy: to "ensure that there are no unilateral changes to the status quo from either side and that we maintain that peace and stability across the Taiwan Strait" (*CNN* 2023).

Given Beijing's long-standing refusal to forswear the use of force or coercion to realize what it calls "reunification," to achieve these objectives the 1979 TRA authorized "defensive" arms sales to Taiwan and declared it U.S. policy "to consider any effort to determine the future of Taiwan by other than peaceful means, including by boycotts or embargoes, a threat to the peace and security of the Western Pacific area and of grave concern to the United States" ("Taiwan Relations Act" 1979).

Meanwhile, the U.S. declaration of an "abiding interest" (Department of State 2022) in the peaceful resolution of cross-Strait differences not only suggests the possibility of U.S. intervention if Beijing were to use "other than peaceful means" against Taiwan, it also suggests that PRC aggression could be a game-changer in other ways. For instance, after what were then the largest-ever PLA military exercises around Taiwan in March 1996, Secretary of State Warren Christopher stated not only that the United States remains committed to "robust unofficial relations" with Taiwan but also that "our 'one China' policy is predicated on the PRC's pursuit of a peaceful resolution of issues between Taipei and Beijing" (Christopher 1996).

2.3.4 Defining Unofficiality

To say U.S. relations with Taiwan are "unofficial" is one thing; to define what "unofficial" – or "robust" – means in practice, and where the effective bounds on "appropriate" policy are, is something entirely different. As Bush notes, "In between the clearly official and clearly unofficial, there are a lot of grey areas." He highlights four factors that affect U.S. decision-making: consideration of national interests, expected reaction from Beijing, Taiwan's own policies, and domestic political pressures. (Bush 2017, 15–18) As Sections 3 and 4 attest, the same basic logic applies to major U.S. democratic allies.

Early examples of U.S. efforts to preserve what Bush refers to as "the façade of unofficiality" included the decision to set up the American Institute in Taiwan (AIT) in 1979 as a private, nongovernmental organization – rather than an official embassy – and the facts that AIT employees for many years had to formally separate from their government agencies before taking up their posts and had to meet their Taiwan counterparts outside government offices (Bush 2017, 15). Although by most measures U.S.-Taiwan engagement has become far more robust and transparent over the past forty-five years, efforts are still made to keep up the officially "unofficial" nature of exchanges. For example, recent high-level meetings involving Taiwan's sitting foreign minister and national security advisor were held not in the U.S. capital of Washington, D.C. but a few miles outside it (*Financial Times* 2024).

Within the broad and amorphous framework of the U.S.' post-1979 "One China policy," U.S. leaders have had ample room to decide practical policies toward Taiwan and the Taiwan Strait. These decisions are fundamentally political. They have been shaped by an unavoidable tension between a desire to support Taiwan's effective autonomy internationally on the one hand, and the twin strategic imperatives to maintain stable ties with the nuclear-armed PRC – today the world's largest trading state, second-largest economy, second-most powerful military, and a U.S. top-three trading partner – while also reducing the risk of Beijing taking destabilizing actions across the Strait on the other.

Analytically, therefore, one must distinguish between the "form" of the U.S.-Taiwan relationship, whereby in officially recognizing only the PRC government the U.S. government since 1979 has adhered to a "One China" policy, and its "substance," whereby U.S. "unofficial" relations with Taiwan have become increasingly robust over time (Bush 2004, 121–22).

In short, U.S. recognition of the PRC in 1979 as the "sole legal government of China" was not tantamount to a U.S. commitment to silence or disinterest about Taiwan or cross-Strait stability; nor did it lock in a particular level or type of engagement with Taipei. On the contrary, over time successive U.S. administrations – often with significant pressure from Congress – have chosen to deepen practical cooperation, including militarily. Seen from Washington, these effective shifts generally have been aimed at maintaining a precarious status quo amid some profound changes, including Taiwan's democratization, a rapidly changing military balance of power, and Beijing's increased coercive pressure against Taipei – especially during periods of DPP rule.

The cumulative effect of irregular internal policy reviews, ad hoc executive decisions, and legislation spearheaded by the U.S. Congress, inter alia, is that U.S. efforts to support Taiwan's international space and peace and stability across the Strait are demonstrably more extensive today than in 1979, 1999, or even 2019. Especially since the 1990s, so, too, are the frequency, level, and nature of bilateral exchanges between government officials and the depth and breadth of military, security, and intelligence cooperation.

Unfortunately, what the overwhelmingly U.S.-centric academic and policy discourse often misses is that key U.S. allies have played a critical support, and at times even leading, role in engaging Taiwan, bolstering its international space, and contributing to peace and stability across the Taiwan Strait.

2.4 The Basic Two-Step Analytical Framework

Inspired by the U.S. case, this study's analytical framework is based on the following judgment: a U.S. ally's (or any foreign government's) effective policy toward Taiwan and the Taiwan Strait is best understood as the combination of two factors: (1) its official position on "One China"; and (2) how the allied government's political leaders have subsequently chosen to operationalize that position in practical terms in the absence of official diplomatic relations with Taiwan. This conceptualization inspires the following straightforward two-step analytical framework:

2.4.1 Step 1: Identify the Government's Official Position on Taiwan's Status

What is the allied government's official position on "One China" as it relates to the sovereignty question? Most fundamentally: upon recognizing the PRC, did the allied government endorse Beijing's claim of sovereignty over Taiwan?

Given Beijing's frequent assertions that the U.S. and its major democratic treaty allies are violating past commitments to the PRC's "one-China principle," whether each government actually endorsed Beijing's claim of sovereignty over Taiwan upon recognizing the PRC is fundamental to any objective analysis of U.S. allies' positions and policies. Indeed, the U.S. case demonstrates how an ambiguous position can be a key enabler of "robust unofficial" relations with Taiwan and how Washington pursues its "practical objective" vis-à-vis the Taiwan Strait. It may also have potential legal implications if China were ever to openly aggress against Taiwan.

In most cases examined in Sections 3 and 4, the allied government's official position on "One China" is formalized in a unilateral declaration or joint communiqué with the PRC. Regardless of the form, the positions themselves are unilateral statements of policy; that is, they are political positions, not consensus or legally binding agreements with or commitments to Beijing. This matters not only in the abstract or when thinking about potential futures, but also because a few cases reveal subtle but noteworthy shifts – even decades after recognizing Beijing.

2.4.2 Step 2: Identify How Leaders Have Chosen to Operationalize That Official Position

In the absence of official diplomatic relations with Taipei, to what extent and how have subsequent generations of political leaders in the allied government developed unofficial relations with Taiwan in terms of concrete policies and official rhetoric, the nature, degree, and extent of bilateral or multilateral engagement and cooperation, and as measured in statements/actions in support of Taiwan's international space and the cross-Strait status quo?

The second step entails a significantly higher empirical hurdle: examining the historical and contemporary record in each case to identify the *practical substance* of the allied government's rhetoric and effective policies toward Taiwan and the Taiwan Strait.

The U.S. example is again illustrative of why this second step is also essential. Though in terms of having major domestic legislation (the *TRA*) at the heart of official policy the U.S. case is sui generis, Washington's evolving approach across successive administrations nevertheless provides a useful baseline and menu of candidate metrics upon which to assess variability in allies' approaches. Though each ally's approach has unique features, in the interest of space, policy relevance, and analytical tractability – especially, the importance of comparing apples to apples – this study's analysis privileges several key indicators (Table 2).

Given the extreme sensitivities in Beijing regarding what its leaders consider to be "at the heart of China's core interests," intentional ambiguity and subtlety permeate U.S. positions and policies vis-à-vis Taiwan and the Taiwan Strait. Unsurprisingly, the same is generally true to even greater degree for U.S. allies and partners – almost all of whom can today be considered objectively "weaker" relative to Beijing in terms of material power and, in several cases, have far

Table 2 Key indicators for assessing operationalization in practical policy

Vis-à-vis Taiwan	• "Rhetorical policy" regarding Taiwan itself; that is, the extent to which and how relations with Taiwan, its importance, and its international space feature in official government rhetoric (including speeches and diplomatic white papers).[3]
	• The existence, nature, frequency, and level of seniority of (de facto) diplomatic and political exchange, including the creation, staffing, and function of representative offices in Taipei
	• The issue areas and policy domains in which the government meaningfully engages Taiwan (e.g., is engagement actually limited to strictly economic and cultural exchange, as Beijing prefers and official rhetoric often suggests?)
	• The extent of security cooperation/signaling (e.g., security dialogues; arms sales)
Vis-à-vis the Taiwan Strait	• "Rhetorical policy" regarding the cross-Strait dispute, e.g., official expressions of concern regarding "peace and stability," calls for "peaceful resolution," and/or opposition to "unilateral changes to the status quo" and "use of force/coercion"
	• Whether the government deploys naval vessels to transit the Taiwan Strait

---

[3] Referring to his experience as AIT Chairman, Bush (2017: 3–5) highlights shifts in "rhetorical policy" – such as introducing a new formulation – as important indicators. For example, after Taiwan's democratic transition the U.S. added "and with the assent of the people of Taiwan" to the long-standing demand that cross-Strait issues be resolved "peacefully."

deeper economic interests vis-à-vis China than the United States. Empirical clarity is further frustrated by the unique circumstances of each case, widely varying domestic politics, the strong preference of all U.S. allies to avoid unnecessarily provoking Beijing on the extremely sensitive "issue" of Taiwan, the tendency of some governments to quietly do more than they are willing to say on-the-record, and the not infrequent public statements by politicians at odds with official policy. Given these challenges, the scholar can only do their best, inevitably imperfect though it may be. Simply put, Step 2 is an inherently messy, but necessary, business.

2.4.3 The Necessity of Both Steps

To enable a complete understanding of U.S. allies' effective policies toward Taiwan and the Taiwan Strait, both steps of the analytical framework are necessary. In this and future studies of these or additional cases, it is extremely important to treat the second question as analytically distinct from the first.

Conflating the two would be problematic in both principle and practice. As the evolution of effective U.S. engagement vis-à-vis Taiwan and the Taiwan Strait after 1979 shows, the form a static, decades-old official position on "One China" takes can be a poor predictor of the future substance of actual policy. Accordingly, scholars should not "prebake" into the analytical framework an assumption of direct or consistent correlation – much less causation – between an allied government's abstract, decades-old official position on Taiwan's status and the extent of its willingness (or lack thereof) to develop robust "unofficial" and practical ties with Taiwan, support its international space, or assert an interest in peace and stability across the Taiwan Strait.

As Sections 3 and 4 demonstrate, some allied governments maintain an official position on "One China" similarly vague to that of the U.S. but choose to severely limit practical engagement with and support for Taiwan. Conversely, some allied governments have shifted official rhetoric on Taiwan's status closer to Beijing's preferences than the United States has but nevertheless adopt relatively forward-leaning policies and rhetoric in support of Taiwan. In short, neglecting either of the two steps risks potentially erroneous prejudgments about a determinative causal link between official position (form) and effective policy (substance) that risks inappropriately skewing the analysis.

3 Indo-Pacific Allies: Japan, South Korea, and Australia

This section examines the significance for Taiwan's international space and cross-Strait dynamics, past and present, of the positions and policies of Japan, the Republic of Korea (below, "ROK" or Korea), and Australia: the

U.S.' three politically closest, most militarily capable, and wealthiest democratic treaty allies in the Western Pacific. All three have significant economic and geopolitical stakes in peace and stability across the Taiwan Strait, as well as important potential roles to play in shaping the peacetime environment and deterring or, potentially, responding to a contingency. Reasons are manifold but generally include: each government's extremely close ties with Washington; geographical proximity to and reliance on commercial trade routes around Taiwan; extensive economic linkages with both China and Taiwan; and, especially for nearby Japan and South Korea, tens of thousands of forward-deployed U.S. military forces on allied soil.[4]

In recent years, all three governments have also become increasingly outspoken on related issues. For example, the joint statement from the historic 2023 Camp David trilateral summit involving the leaders of Japan, Korea, and the United States included the following language: "We reaffirm the importance of peace and stability across the Taiwan Strait as an indispensable element of security and prosperity in the international community." Yet it also noted – vaguely – that "There is no change in our basic positions on Taiwan, and we call for a peaceful resolution of cross-Strait issues" (White House 2023b). Almost exactly one year earlier, Australia's foreign minister had issued a joint statement with her U.S. and Japanese counterparts similarly "reaffirm[ing] their commitment to maintaining peace and stability across the Taiwan Strait," and vaguely noting that "There is no change in the respective one China policies, where applicable, and basic positions of Australia, Japan, or the United States" (White House 2022).

In their respective normalization communiques with Beijing, the governments of Japan (1972), Australia (1972), and Korea (1992) each recognized the PRC as the "sole legal government of China." Nevertheless, each also rejected significant pressure to recognize the PRC's unilateral claim of sovereignty over Taiwan. Instead, all three governments adopt what is effectively a distinct version of the Canadian formula, vaguely referencing Beijing's claim without endorsing it and thereby avoiding a clear position on Taiwan's status. In this regard, all three governments' official positions on "one China" resemble the U.S. position (1979) and are fundamentally distinct from Beijing's "one-China principle," an essential condition of which is its claim that Taiwan is part of the PRC.

Despite these similarly vague official positions on Taiwan's status, however, how elected leaders in Japan, Australia, and South Korea have chosen to operationalize their effective policies vis-à-vis Taiwan and the Taiwan Strait

---

[4] The United States regularly rotates forces through Australia and is currently constructing facilities to expand rotations and visits by aircraft and naval vessels. E.g., *Reuters* 2024.

over the ensuing years evince noteworthy variability – both across and within these cases. This demonstrates the political contingency at the heart of the "One China" framework's operationalization in international politics. Each ally's vague, decades-old abstract position is far from determinative of specific policy outcomes. Of these three cases, Japan has been a particularly significant trailblazer in stretching the effective bounds of what is possible – in several regards even drafting pages of a playbook that the United States and others would later follow.

3.1 Japan

Given Japan's status as a close neighbor, economic partner, and former colonizer of Taiwan that maintained significant links with Taiwan after 1949, both Beijing and Taipei have long considered Tokyo the second most important external player in cross-Strait dynamics after the United States. Today, Japan is not only the world's third-largest economy and a major political and security player in the Indo-Pacific. It is also both China's and Taiwan's third-largest trading partner. Japan's geographical proximity – for example, the inhabited island of Yonaguni is located just 70 miles east of Taiwan and 200 miles from mainland China – and the U.S. military's massive naval, air, and ground force presence on Japanese soil make Japan's policies a critical variable in Taiwan's international space and cross-Strait peace and stability. Given Japan's relative significance, this study discusses it at greater length than other cases in this section.

3.1.1 The Origins and Post-1972 Evolution of Japan's Approach to Taiwan

In signing a separate peace treaty with the ROC government in 1952 and seeking out a possible "two Chinas" or "one China, one Taiwan" solution to the cross-Strait dispute, during the early Cold War Japan's leaders firmly aligned with Washington. Nevertheless, Nixon's shocking July 1971 announcement that he planned to visit China the following year, about which Japan's prime minister had mere minutes' advance warning, caused Tokyo to significantly accelerate the increase of its unofficial engagement of the PRC. Tokyo switched diplomatic recognition from Taipei to Beijing more than six years earlier than Washington. Although the September 1972 Japan–PRC normalization communique meant the end of official Japan–ROC diplomatic relations, four decisions by Japanese leaders immediately before and after carried profound long-term consequences for Taiwan's international space and cross-Strait stability.

First, for historical, geopolitical, and geographical reasons it was especially meaningful that Japan's government refused to explicitly endorse Beijing's claim of sovereignty over Taiwan, despite a clear desire among Japanese leaders to expand economic and political engagement with the PRC (and significant political and business pressure to do so). Ultimately, in the 1972 communique Japan recognized the PRC as the "sole legal government of China" but merely expressed its "full understanding and respect" of Beijing's claim of sovereignty over Taiwan (Gaimushō 1972).[5] It did not endorse that position.

Second, even after recognizing the PRC Tokyo insisted on maintaining de facto, if officially "nongovernmental," ties with Taiwan by establishing in Taipei a euphemistically named "Exchange Association" (*kōryū kyōkai*) to serve as a kind of de facto embassy. This was an extraordinarily significant development. An Australian secret cable three months later revealed that Beijing had been deeply concerned that Japan's move would set a precedent for other U.S. allies to follow (Doran and Lee 2002, 828). That concern proved well-founded. Indeed, the so-called "Japan Formula" set the precedent for, inter alia, the euphemistically named foreign representative offices that the United States and other U.S. allies would establish in Taipei years later (Hirakawa 2006; Liff 2022b).

Third, in institutionalizing in 1973 a pipeline for frequent exchanges between ruling party legislators close to their respective governments – the Japanese Diet Members' Council for Japan-ROC Relations (*Nikka giin kondankai*) – Japanese politicians carved out space for meaningful, if ostensibly nongovernmental, diplomacy and dialogue with leaders in Taiwan, despite the absence of official relations. It was another trailblazing move.

Fourth, as discussed in greater detail below, by the mid-1970s Japan publicly adopted an official position calling for "peaceful resolution" (*heiwateki kaiketsu*) of the cross-Strait dispute.

In all four of the aforementioned decisions, Tokyo acted years before the United States had even recognized Beijing, much less established AIT or sent its first post-switch congressional delegation to Taiwan.

Why did PRC leaders grudgingly "allow" Japan to circumvent Beijing's initial conditions for diplomatic normalization as it concerned Taiwan? The answer is politics or, more precisely, shifting geopolitical and economic interests. In the 1970s and 1980s, Beijing's twin desires to work with the United States and Japan to contain the Soviet Union and receive from Washington and

---

[5] As noted in Section 2, the 1951 San Francisco Peace Treaty saw Japan "renounce[] all right, title and claim to Formosa and the Pescadores" but said nothing about to which entity sovereignty over them was subsequently transferred. This ambiguity was not explicitly resolved in Japan's subsequent peace agreements with either the ROC (1952) or the PRC (1978).

Tokyo massive economic investment and knowhow trumped other concerns. The PRC's grudging consent to omit Taiwan from all three post-1972 "political documents" that it regularly identifies as "defining" Japan–PRC relations further consolidated this effective status quo, which basically persists to this day. (Liff 2022b) A half-century after the 1972 communique, Japan's official position on the sovereignty question remains that it has no legal position (Matsuda 2020, 247).

Though Japan's government today continues to state publicly that its relations with Taiwan are "non-governmental and practical" (*hiseifukan no jitsumu kankei*) (Gaimushō 2023a, 51), the idea that the relationship is exclusively economic and cultural is a convenient fiction. Especially since the 1990s, Japan and Taiwan have carried out incrementally more meaningful quasi-diplomacy and cooperation through, inter alia, the de facto embassies on each other's soil and frequent exchanges of ruling party politicians. For instance, in the twenty-first century many former Japanese prime ministers and former Cabinet ministers have visited Taiwan after resigning their positions. Meanwhile, economic and people-to-people ties are also robust; in recent years, Japan has also been Taiwan's fourth-largest source of FDI (Ministry of Economic Affairs 2023).

As for Japan's policies vis-a-vis cross-Strait peace and stability, for most of the latter half of the twentieth century Tokyo effectively delegated deterrence to Taipei and Washington. Nevertheless, Japan contributed indirectly by allowing the United States to forward-deploy tens of thousands of U.S. military personnel on Japanese soil – especially in nearby Okinawa – and through rhetorical signals at key moments. For example, in a 1969 U.S.-Japan summit-level communique, Japan's prime minister unilaterally stated "that the maintenance of peace and security in the Taiwan area was also a most important factor for the security of Japan" (*New York Times* 1969). Even after recognizing Beijing three years later, the Japanese government repeatedly asserted an interest in "peaceful resolution" of cross-Strait differences (Fujita 2021). Its refusal to endorse Beijing's claim of sovereignty over Taiwan also enabled Tokyo to maintain a definition of "the Far East" – a key phrase in the 1960 U.S.-Japan mutual security treaty – that includes "the Taiwan area." After 1972, Beijing pressured Tokyo to change the definition but Tokyo refused[6] (Liff 2022a, 136–41).

Major PLA military exercises in March 1996 in and around the Taiwan Strait included missiles splashing down in waters near Japanese islands. These

---

[6] The "Far East" clause (Article VI) of the security treaty stipulates that U.S. bases in Japan are, inter alia, for "contributing to ... the maintenance of international peace and security in the Far East." The phrase "Far East" was defined vaguely. After Japan and China normalized diplomatic relations, Beijing demanded that Japan state clearly that Taiwan was not included in the definition of the "Far East." Tokyo refused.

provocative exercises, coupled with new frictions on the Korean Peninsula owing to North Korea's nuclear weapons program, contributed to Tokyo's decision to negotiate new bilateral "Guidelines for Defense Cooperation" with its U.S. ally. These guidelines noted the possibility of allied cooperation in a "situation in areas surrounding Japan," a vague phrase that left it deliberately ambiguous whether Japan might provide "rear-area" (read: mostly logistical) support to U.S. forces if a cross-Strait conflict occurred. (Barring an attack on Japan itself, however, a JSDF combat role remained off the table.) Although extremely limited, some unofficial security links developed subsequently. For example, in 2003 Tokyo began quietly dispatching a (retired) JSDF officer to Taipei to serve as a de facto defense attaché. And in 2005 it issued a joint statement with its U.S. ally identifying "peaceful resolution" of the cross-Strait dispute as a "common strategic objective" (Liff 2022a, 141–44).

3.1.2 The Contemporary Situation

In recent years, the ambiguity of Japan's unchanged 1972 official position has enabled a substantial expansion of mutually beneficial cooperation, significant flexibility in nominally "nongovernmental" engagements, official rhetoric more supportive of Taiwan's international space, and more frequent expressions of concern about cross-Strait peace and stability. For example, Taipei and Tokyo have signed numerous bilateral agreements and launched annual maritime cooperation dialogues involving representatives from the two sides' de facto embassies and government officials (Shimizu 2020). Meanwhile, exchanges between parliamentarians have become more frequent, higher-level, and increasingly substantive; for instance, visits by Japanese Diet members now often involve meetings with Taiwan's sitting president. This was symbolically demonstrated when a 31-member delegation of *Nikkakon* members representing all Japan's political parties (except Japan's Communist Party) not only attended President Lai's May 2024 inauguration but was also invited to a luncheon with both Lai and Vice President Hsiao Bi-khim (*Fōkasu Taiwan*, 2024).

Dialogue on security issues has also increased, albeit primarily through legislative channels. For example, the LDP and DPP held the first-ever inter-ruling party security dialogue in 2021. In 2023 then-LDP vice president (and former prime minister) Asō Tarō became the highest-ranking ruling party leader to ever visit Taiwan. Though representing his party and not Japan's government, Asō's visit included bold rhetoric on the threat to Taiwan and a meeting with President Tsai (*Kyodo* 2023a).

A shifting political calculus in Tokyo also means some steps previously dismissed as too provocative or connotative of "official" exchange or recognition are now judged "appropriate." For example, in 2017 Japan dispatched the highest-level government representative since 1972 – a deputy minister – to visit Taiwan and added "Japan-Taiwan" to the Exchange Association's official name. This followed a series of decisions after 2012 to stop referring to Taiwan in Japan's official diplomatic bluebook as merely an "economic region" and instead grant it political status and agency as an "extremely crucial partner and an important friend, with which [Japan] shares universal values." In recent years, Japan's Foreign Ministry also has congratulated Taiwan's president-elect after democratic elections and abandoned the practice of placing scare quotes around "president" (Gaimushō 2023a, 51; Liff 2022b).

In terms of Taiwan's international space, Japan's leaders now regularly express support for Taipei's participation in both international organizations for which statehood is not a requirement and the Comprehensive and Progressive Trans-Pacific Partnership – a major multilateral trade agreement. Tokyo has also ramped up coordination with the United States and other U.S. allies. For example, in 2019 Japan became the first non-founding member of the Global Cooperation and Training Framework (GCTF), started by the United States and Taiwan in 2015 as a "platform through which Taiwan could contribute to global problem solving and share its expertise with partners across the region" (Liff 2022b). And the 2023 G7 summit – of which Japan was host – released a statement calling for "Taiwan's meaningful participation in international organizations" (G7 2023a).

Regarding cross-Strait peace and stability, recent years have witnessed a remarkable mainstreaming in Japan of concerns about the risk a potential conflict poses to Japan. Following the April 2021 U.S.-Japan joint statement's first-ever summit-level reference to "the importance of peace and stability across the Taiwan Strait," the allies have worked to multilateralize similar expressions of concern and, consistent with Japan's half-century-old position, calls for "peaceful resolution of cross-Strait issues" (e.g., White House 2021b). Japan's authoritative national security and defense documents now regularly emphasize linkages between cross-Strait peace, Japan's own security, and the stability of "the international community" (e.g., Bōeishō 2021). Japanese media have even claimed that the United States and Japan are developing their first-ever classified joint operational plan for a Taiwan contingency (*Mainichi Shimbun* 2023). Although an alleged plan's mere existence would not indicate a concrete, much less binding, commitment to take any particular action in a conflict, it nevertheless suggests unprecedentedly severe concerns in Tokyo about cross-Strait stability and willingness to bolster deterrence jointly with the United States. In 2023 and 2024, Japan even reportedly took the historic steps of dispatching a civilian Ministry of Defense official to the Exchange Association in Taipei, sailing a destroyer through the Taiwan Strait, and holding a joint coast guard search and rescue drill (*Kyodo* 2023b; *Yomiuri* 2024).

Although all the aforementioned developments demonstrate practically meaningful shifts in Japan's concerns about and approaches toward Taiwan and cross-Strait peace and stability, it is important to recognize that significant caution still obtains in Tokyo out of concern for possible backlash from Beijing, Japan's next-door neighbor and top trading partner. For example, despite being widely considered Taiwan's most important international partner after the United States, and France, Germany, Canada, Australia, and many other U.S. allies having dispatched their first Cabinet-level official to Taiwan by 1993, Japan did not take a similar step until 2017 – and only at the deputy minister level. Taiwan's sitting president does not "transit" through Japan, as recent presidents have done through the United States. And although it has some new holes, the effective political firewall limiting direct military-military or security engagement between governments remains significant. Widespread media hype to the contrary, Japan has not carried out intergovernmental "2+2" security dialogues or seriously considered a "Japanese TRA." Nor has it sold military platforms to Taiwan. And contrary to widespread claims since 2021 that Tokyo has somehow committed to defend Taiwan, the Japanese government continues to adopt a posture best summed up as strategic ambiguity and to view deterrence primarily through a U.S.-Japan alliance lens (Liff 2022a).

In sum, this brief survey reveals the extent to which – even as Japan's official position on Taiwan remains frozen in 1972 and its government continues to claim only "working relations at the non-governmental level" (Gaimushō 2023a, 51) – the "line" separating what is politically acceptable versus unacceptable to leaders in Tokyo vis-à-vis Taiwan is subjectively defined and subject to Japanese leaders' evolving interpretations of international and domestic political dynamics. By any objective measure, the degree and nature of Tokyo's engagement with Taipei, and with issues related to the Taiwan Strait, have changed in both symbolically and practically significant ways over the past half-century. Nevertheless, it is also important not to exaggerate the pace, scale, and significance of these changes. For this study, what matter most are Japan's trail-blazing steps in the 1970s and the remarkable flexibility in Japan's effective Taiwan policy and rhetoric, all of which remains – in the Japanese government's official political judgment – fully consistent with the 1972 Japan–PRC communique.

3.2 Australia

Among the three allied cases in this section, Australia stands out for its distance from Taiwan (2500 miles, compared to 600 for Korea and 70 for Japan) and relatively small population.[7] Even so, Australia is an important case. It maintains very close political and security ties with its U.S. treaty ally, is cultivating a burgeoning security relationship with Japan, and has significant trade with Taiwan. At the same time, robust economic ties with China – far and away Australia's top trading partner for nearly two decades – have been key drivers of Australia's remarkable quarter-century of uninterrupted economic growth before the COVID-19 pandemic.

3.2.1 The Origins and Post-1972 Evolution of Australia's Approach to Taiwan

After the PRC was established in October 1949, Australia joined the United States and most other non-Communist nations in not recognizing the new Communist regime. Skepticism about and frictions with the authoritarian KMT regime in Taiwan, however, contributed to Canberra's decision not to establish an embassy in Taipei until 1966. Nevertheless, Australia did support the 1954 U.S.-ROC mutual defense treaty and the ROC maintained an embassy in Canberra and consulates in Sydney and Melbourne (Doran and Lee 2002, 86; Klintworth 1993, 1–6).

Australian skepticism of the ROC regime after 1949 should not be mistaken for a judgment that Taiwan belonged to the PRC, however. On the contrary, before 1972 Australian governments explored possibilities for "two Chinas," "one China, one Taiwan," and self-determination for "Formosa" and "the people of Taiwan" (Atkinson 2013, chap. 2; Doran and Lee 2002, xxii–xxvi). Atkinson sums up Australia's goal during the early Cold War as "centered on an effort to create an independent Taiwan, either Taiwanese-majority controlled or an independent Republic of China on Taiwan ruled by the Chinese Nationalists and the mainland Chinese minority." In other words, many in Canberra hoped for "a government in Taipei that would assert de jure independent status for Taiwan – whether controlled by the Taiwanese majority or Chinese Nationalists that had dropped their claim" to the mainland. Indeed, in 1970 Australia's UN representative declared that Canberra's "objective" was to allow the PRC to participate in the UN "while preserving separate membership, under whatever name, for the [ROC] and Taiwan" (Atkinson 2013, 2–3; 30–34; 38).

A secret February 1971 Cabinet decision stated Australia's objective plainly: "It should be Australian policy that the interests of the people of Taiwan be upheld and that Taiwan should be preserved as a separate entity and as a member of the United Nations if it so desires." Throughout 1971 and 1972

---

[7] Despite doubling between 1972 and 2024, Australia's population today (~27 million) is 22 percent and 52 percent of Japan's and South Korea's, respectively.

the Australian government repeatedly tried to defend the ROC's membership in the UN General Assembly and pursued an "effective 'two Chinas' formula" (Doran and Lee 2002, xvii–xxix; 395).

After Nixon's February 1972 visit to Beijing, Canberra followed Japan and many others in switching official recognition from the ROC to the PRC. Nevertheless, Australian negotiators rejected Beijing's demand that Canberra recognize the PRC's position that Taiwan was "a province of China." In the December 1972 Australia–PRC communique, Australia adopted the closest modification of the Canadian formula that Beijing would accept – "acknowledg[ing] the position of the Chinese government that Taiwan is a province of the People's Republic of China," without endorsing Beijing's claim. (Canberra considered Canada's "take note of" and its "acknowledge" – the word the United States had used several months earlier in the Shanghai Communique – as basically synonymous.) A secret cable even highlighted "no direct grammatical connexion ... between the territorial issue of Taiwan and the removal of official representation." Canberra's refusal to endorse Beijing's position was no accident. The government's position held that "the removal of representation is a necessary consequence of recognizing the PRC Government as the sole legal Government of China and has nothing to do with the territorial issue of Taiwan" (Doran and Lee 2002, 827).

After 1972, it would thenceforth be left to Australia's political leaders to determine how to operationalize Canberra's ambiguous official position on "One China" and to define what it would mean *in practice* for "unofficial" Australia-Taiwan relations. The beginning was inauspicious for Taiwan. Against the backdrop of U.S.-PRC rapprochement and strategic realignment against the Soviet Union, Canberra unilaterally imposed numerous, strict restraints on exchanges with Taiwan, effectively limiting bilateral engagement to "the bare minimum required to sustain trade" (Atkinson 2013, 41–47).

By the 1980s, however, Taiwan's blistering GDP growth incentivized Australian leaders to engage Taipei more robustly as an economic and trading partner and source of investment. Furthermore, Beijing's globally televised, deadly crackdown on protesters in June 1989 – most famously in Tiananmen Square – contrasted sharply with Taiwan's end of martial law and rapid democratization. Australian Foreign Minister Gareth Evans predicted that "Tiananmen" would have consequences for foreign governments' ties with Taiwan, suggesting – presciently – that countries "that already trade widely with Taiwan[] may feel less inhibited in increasing their contacts with Taiwan in other areas, though stopping short of switching diplomatic recognition" (Evans 1989, 282).

Sure enough, Australia gradually loosened self-imposed restrictions on exchanges with Taiwan; for example, staffing its de facto representative office in Taipei – the euphemistically named "Australian Commerce and Industry Office" (ACIO) – with government officials "on leave." Australia–Taiwan ties continued to deepen in the 1990s, as Canberra allowed "unofficial" ministerial visits and direct government contacts, sent a DFAT official to head ACIO, lifted restrictions on sales of nonlethal weapons to Taiwan, and signed multiple bilateral agreements with Taipei. In 1992, Canberra gave Taipei permission to open a Taipei Economic and Cultural Office (TECO) – a significant upgrade over the vague and euphemistic "Far East Trading Company" name given to its earlier representative offices in Melbourne and Sydney. Canberra allowed TECO staff to have direct contacts with Australian officials and granted them diplomatic privileges and immunities. TECO even began issuing visas with an "ROC" stamp. This de facto upgrading of Australia's relations with Taiwan continued with the first "unofficial" Australian ministerial visit to Taiwan in 1992 (Atkinson 2013, 47–57; Klintworth 1993, 109–14).

Throughout this period support for Taiwan's international engagement and cross-Strait peace and stability also grew. For example, Australia supported Taiwan's involvement in the GATT and APEC (Atkinson 2013, 55–56). And in 1996, Australia and Japan were the only two regional governments to publicly support the U.S. response to the PLA's large-scale military exercises in the weeks leading up to Taiwan's first-ever direct presidential election. Canberra also called on Beijing and Taipei to "resolve differences without a resort to military force" (MacKerras 2000).

In aggregate, these incremental shifts marked the late 1980s/early 1990s as a practical inflection point in Australia's officially "unofficial" ties with Taiwan. Importantly, these shifts all occurred nearly two decades after the Australia–PRC normalization communique, and without any changes to Canberra's ambiguous official 1972 position on "One China."

In short, by the end of the twentieth century Australia had in practical ways begun treating Taiwan as a political entity distinct from the PRC for all but official political and diplomatic purposes. Writing in 1993, Klintworth summed up Australia's position thus: "officially one China, and unofficially one China and one Republic of China on Taiwan. It is a two Chinas policy presented as one China, the kind of practical policy approach that Australia has sought to implement since 1949" (Klintworth 1993, 132).

3.2.2 The Contemporary Situation

The July 2020 U.S.–Australia "2+2" (AUSMIN) statement was a very public, high-level reflection of how much views of Taiwan in Canberra have changed since the Cold War. It contained a full paragraph about Taiwan, which granted

Taipei political status and agency by noting "Taiwan's important role in the Indo-Pacific." It committed Canberra and Washington to "maintain strong unofficial ties with Taiwan; to support its membership in international organizations where statehood is not a prerequisite" and its "meaningful participation" where it is; and to "strengthen [their] ... resolve to support Taiwan." Lastly, it also stated that "any resolution of cross-Strait differences should be peaceful and according to the will of the people on both sides, without resorting to threats or coercion" (DFAT 2020).

In the years since, Canberra has released additional joint statements with the United States, France, and other U.S. allies making similar calls. It continues to quietly carry out Taiwan Strait transits with naval vessels and followed Japan to become the GCTF's fourth official member in 2021. It has also reportedly increased engagement with the United States to consider possible coordination/cooperation in the event of a Taiwan contingency. Perhaps most famously, in 2021 Defense Minister Peter Dutton made global headlines when he stated in an unscripted moment that "It would be inconceivable that we wouldn't support the US" if the United States came to Taiwan's aid in a conflict (McGregor 2023). In terms of political and economic exchange, since 2020 cross-party delegations from Australia's Parliament have increased and two-way trade has tripled. Australia became Taiwan's top energy and mineral supplier, and Taiwan became Australia's fourth-largest destination for exports and fifth-largest trading partner (*Taiwan Today* 2023).

Though these developments are undoubtedly significant, a comprehensive look at Australia's post–Cold War approach to Taiwan reveals that the trajectory is neither inevitably linear nor unidirectional. As in other cases, the available evidence suggests that Australia's political leaders remain cautious about engaging Taiwan in several areas – sometimes even more so than in the past. And consideration of how China – far and away Australia's top trading partner – may react appears to loom large in Canberra's calculus.

A few examples: Although Australian ministers with limited portfolios – for example, economics, trade, and/or energy – began visiting Taiwan in the mid-1990s, such public visits ceased after 2012. Whereas close neighbor New Zealand signed an FTA with Taiwan in 2013, Australia reportedly abandoned efforts to do so after warnings from Beijing, making Taiwan Australia's largest trading partner with which it does not have an FTA. Nor does Canberra appear as openly supportive of Taiwan joining CPTPP as Japan. Security-wise, Dutton's global-headline-generating 2021 comment has not since been repeated. And Canberra reportedly turned down requests from Taipei to exchange de facto defense attachés (McGregor 2023).

In short, there is an observable deepening of Australia's engagement with and rhetorical support of Taiwan in some contexts and domains, but greater caution in others, especially bilaterally. This is hardly surprising or unique to Canberra. Rather, it is a testament to the complicated tradeoffs that all governments face when balancing interests vis-à-vis Taipei and Beijing. Simply put, with an official position on "One China" unchanged since 1972, the practical operationalization of the stated goals and means by which Canberra pursues "strong unofficial ties" with Taiwan have always been largely what Australian leaders judge they should be. Political calculation of national interests looms large.

The administration of Labor MP Anthony Albanese (2022–) is the latest to try to strike a balance as it seeks to improve ties with Beijing following a historically bad five-year period in Australia–PRC relations. As for the Taiwan Strait, administration officials have emphasized Australia's role as convincing others to "lower the heat on any potential conflict." In a major speech in April 2023, Minister for Foreign Affairs Penny Wong highlighted that "war over Taiwan would be catastrophic for all," adding,

> We know that there would be no real winners, and we know maintaining the status quo is comprehensively superior to any alternative. It will be challenging, requiring both reassurance and deterrence, but it is the proposition most capable of averting conflict and enabling the region to live in peace and prosperity. (DFAT 2023b)

3.3 Republic of Korea

In 1992, South Korea became the last U.S. treaty ally in Asia to switch recognition from the ROC to the PRC. Seoul's policies today remain an important factor in U.S.-led international efforts to support Taiwan's international space and cross-Strait stability. Reasons include Korea's geographical proximity, with Jeju Island only 600 miles away; close security alliance with Washington and hosting of 28,000 forward-deployed U.S. military personnel; deep economic links with China, and to a much lesser but still significant extent, Taiwan, Seoul's fifth-largest trading partner; and an immense and potentially existential stake in regional peace and stability, especially given that 90 percent of its maritime trade passes through the Taiwan Strait and feared linkages between cross-Strait peace and stability on the Korean Peninsula.

3.3.1 The Origins and Post-1992 Evolution of South Korea's Approach to Taiwan

After the Soviet Union's collapse (1991) and the ROK's and DPRK's simultaneous admissions into the United Nations (1992), it was, ironically, Seoul's first democratic government that switched diplomatic recognition from the rapidly democratizing ROC to the communist-led PRC. Adopting the by then well-worn playbook of Canada, Japan, Australia, and the United States, in the August 1992 ROK–PRC normalization communique Seoul accepted "that the PRC [is] the sole legal Government of China," but refused to endorse Beijing's claim of sovereignty over Taiwan. Instead, Seoul allowed only that it "respects the position of the Chinese side that there is but one China and Taiwan is part of China" – without taking a clear position itself.[8]

Seoul's decision in 1992 not to endorse Beijing's "one-China principle" was no accident. In his 2003 memoir, Korea's foreign minister during the negotiations notes that Beijing pressured Seoul to explicitly recognize Taiwan as part of the PRC. But it refused to do so. (Lee 2003, 215–16) Also important: Even after severing official diplomatic relations with the ROC, President Roh Tae-woo (1988–1993) called for Seoul to honor its historically close ties with Taipei by establishing "the highest level of unofficial relations" that would be both "substantive" and the "best" possible (Chen 2008) – an implicit recognition of the distinction between form and substance.

As the last-mover among major U.S. treaty allies, after 1992 Seoul had numerous models and precedents from which to choose when deciding what those "unofficial relations" would look like in practice. Or its leaders could establish their own. And they did, at least initially. Seoul became the only U.S. ally to name its representative office in Taipei a "mission" – a term with clear diplomatic connotations. It also maintained some military contacts with Taiwan, including a military officer exchange program that continued until Beijing forced its cancellation in 2011 (*Taipei Times* 2011). And the ROK military reportedly even continued to station a "liaison officer" at Korea's Taipei-based mission (Cho 2021).

3.3.2 The Contemporary Situation

Those notable developments aside, with the benefit of 30-plus years of hindsight the practical substance of Korea's effective Taiwan policy today appears to have fallen short of Roh's ambitious call for "the highest level of unofficial relations." Seoul's public engagement with Taiwan and advocacy for Taiwan's international space and, at least until recently, cross-Strait peace and stability, have been relatively limited – even when compared to the other cases in this section, to say nothing of its U.S. ally.

Although Seoul and Taipei today are top-five trading partners (ITA 2023) and hold working-level dialogues, ROK leaders appear far more reluctant than their

---

[8] Unofficial English translation of Korean-language version from Lee and Liff, 2023, 57.

counterparts in Tokyo, Canberra, and several other major U.S. democratic allies to speak out in support of Taiwan or its international space. This holds even in the case of those international organizations where Beijing previously "allowed" Taiwan to participate as an observer – such as the World Health Assembly. Furthermore, recent ROK leader rhetoric and official diplomatic and defense white papers have conspicuously avoided substantive discussions of Korea–Taiwan relations, Taiwan's international space, or ROK interests in either. Nor, and also in contrast to Canberra and Tokyo, does ROK official government rhetoric express a clear interest in deepening "nongovernmental" ties with Taiwan or supporting its "meaningful participation" in international organizations.[9] And in terms of political exchange, prominent visits by political leaders to Taipei are rare: The focus remains quasi-annual visits by the ROK-Taiwan Parliamentary Friendship Association (e.g., *South China Morning Post* 2023). Also distinct from several other U.S. allies, neither the Korean government nor Korea's National Assembly has unambiguously expressed its support for Taiwan's international space. (Lee and Liff 2023)

Taiwan's leaders appear to have taken note of Korea's reluctance to publicly risk Beijing's ire by engaging on these issues. In her 2021 National Day speech thanking "democratic friends willing to stand up for us," President Tsai did not reference Seoul, but did mention Tokyo, Canberra, the EU, the G7, NATO, and Washington. (Tsai 2021) Taiwan's foreign minister later publicly complained that "Korea has inked an economic agreement or engaged in related negotiations with all of its top 10 trading partners except Taiwan" (*Korea Times* 2024).

Regarding cross-Strait frictions the story was largely the same until 2021, when Biden and President Moon Jae-in released a joint statement that – while conspicuously avoiding any reference to Taiwan itself – included a sentence "emphasiz[ing] the importance of preserving peace and stability in the Taiwan Strait" (White House 2021c). While still avoiding specific reference to "Taiwan" in official statements, the unabashedly "pro-U.S." and "pro-Japan" Yoon Suk-yeol administration (2022–) has gone even further, flagging the "importance of peace and stability in the Taiwan Strait" as both an international issue and one linked to "peace and stability of the Korean Peninsula" (ROK Government 2022, 28). At the U.S.-Japan-Korea trilateral summit in August 2023 Seoul for the first time signed on to a statement calling for

---

[9] A survey of ROK diplomatic and defense white papers between 2008 and 2022 finds substantive references to Taiwan or cross-Strait vicissitudes rare, banal, and matter-of-fact. None contains a section devoted to Korea–Taiwan relations or expressions of *ROK concerns* about cross-Strait vicissitudes, opposition to coercion, support for Taiwan's international space, or interest in the bilateral relationship. Available at: www.mnd.go.kr/cop/pblictn/selectPublicationsUser.do?siteId=mnd&componentId=14&categoryId=15&pageIndex=1&id=mnd_040501000000 and www.mofa.go.kr/www/brd/m_4105/list.do)

"peaceful resolution" of cross-Strait issues – adopting language Tokyo and Washington have used for decades (White House 2023b). Although Korean leaders appear to still be reluctant to issue statements expressing support for Taiwan itself and/or its international space, since 2021 leaders in Seoul have begun aligning official rhetoric on the importance of cross-Strait peace and stability with that of other U.S. allies.

Even so, Seoul has long quietly resisted U.S. calls for the U.S.-ROK alliance to play a more robust regional security role, or to hold talks about possible coordination in an off-Peninsula contingency over Taiwan. Facing an existential threat from its nuclear-armed northern neighbor, since the Korean War – which has never officially ended – Seoul's long-standing preference has been to keep the alliance's strategic and operational focus on the Korean Peninsula while also avoiding rhetoric or policies that risk unnecessarily antagonizing China – on whose economy Korea is highly dependent and whose cooperation is necessary to address Seoul's manifold concerns about North Korea (Liff 2024; NEAR 2023, 57–58).

Although some scholars (e.g., Mastro and Cho 2022; Park 2022) now call for the ROK to support the U.S. military defending Taiwan through "rear-area" (noncombat) support of the sort that Japan has publicly considered since the mid-1990s, this concept is new to the US-ROK alliance and not something for which the allies have traditionally trained. Despite some recent claims to the contrary, there does not appear to be much mainstream political support in Seoul for this kind of cooperation, or even for U.S. forces in Korea to play a role in the event of a cross-Strait contingency. Public rhetoric from high-ranking Yoon government officials – including the president himself – has consistently emphasized that Seoul's priority both for its military and for the U.S.-ROK alliance is deterring a possible North Korean provocation (e.g., *CNN* 2023; Liff 2024).

3.4 Conclusion

Recent developments demonstrate the extent to which worsening cross-Strait frictions have become – arguably for the first time – a shared foreign policy concern of the U.S. three wealthiest and most militarily capable democratic treaty allies in the Western Pacific. Less obviously, they also demonstrate the importance of clarifying the allies' intentionally vague rhetoric regarding One China policies and basic positions on Taiwan, as well as the difference between form and substance.

In negotiating their respective normalization communiques, Tokyo, Canberra, and Seoul all adopted a version of the Canadian Formula – refusing to endorse Beijing's claim of sovereignty over Taiwan. Yet each case study reveals that these ambiguous and abstract official positions neither locked in nor were particularly predictive of what the *substance* of each ally's subsequent approach vis-à-vis Taiwan and the Taiwan Strait would be in the decades following. On the contrary, the variability across and within these three cases evinces how each government enjoys significant flexibility to operationalize its effective Taiwan policy in accordance with political leaders' evolving interpretations of national interests and perceived trade-offs vis-à-vis relations with Beijing. Indeed, short of a widely understood red line of officially recognizing Taiwan, the bounds of each government's acceptable engagement with and policy toward Taiwan and the Strait have been largely up to successive political leaders to determine.

Both historically and today, among these three cases Japan can be considered the most forward-leaning in terms of political, economic, and people-to-people engagement with Taiwan. Even so, government leaders in Tokyo consistently demonstrate caution in areas less controversial for some other U.S. allies such as Australia. South Korea, meanwhile, stands out among major US treaty allies for its reluctance to speak out in support of Taiwan's international space. It also – at least publicly – avoids suggesting even the possibility of a role for the U.S.-ROK alliance in a cross-Strait contingency. In making relevant policy judgments, political leaders remain ever-mindful of risks of backlash from China, which, despite recent frictions, continues to be all three allies' top trading partner. For Seoul in particular, Beijing also remains a uniquely essential partner in addressing concerns related to North Korea, and fears of possible simultaneous contingencies on both the Korean Peninsula and across the Taiwan Strait loom large.

4 European Allies and Partners: The UK, France, Germany, the EU, and NATO

This section begins by analyzing the significance for Taiwan's international space and cross-Strait dynamics, past and present, of the positions and policies of the United Kingdom (UK), France, and Germany. These three countries are the U.S. most populous and militarily capable democratic treaty allies in Europe, as well as the region's three largest national economies. Coupled with each country's extensive economic links with China, these traits ensure that – despite their geographic distance – their policies and positions are important factors in Taiwan's international space, cross-Strait peace and stability, and U.S. response options in a crisis. Each has also played significant and largely underappreciated historical roles in enabling the ambiguous "One China" framework and, by extension, Taiwan's international space. And all three have adjusted their respective approaches to Taiwan and cross-Strait issues in response to political vicissitudes.

This section's second half examines two important and globally unique cases headquartered in Western Europe: the European Union (EU) and North Atlantic Treaty Organization (NATO). Although neither is a nation-state nor a U.S. treaty ally government, per se, the case for their inclusion in this study is compelling. The EU is the world's third-largest economy, China's top trading partner, and accounts for the second-largest share of global trade. Twenty-three of the EU's twenty-seven democratic member countries, including the eight largest national economies, are also U.S. NATO allies. Not only does the EU have its own official position on and policy vis-à-vis "One China," it also maintains a large representative office in Taiwan, for which it is the top source of external investment. Of particular interest to this study, since 2019 political leaders of the EU's constituent entities (especially the European Commission and European Parliament) have embraced an increasingly assertive political role on China- and Indo-Pacific-related matters. One consequence is an unprecedented degree of attention on and outspokenness concerning Taiwan- and Taiwan Strait–related issues.

The EU case study is followed by a brief assessment of NATO, a multilateral collective defense pact and alliance organization which binds thirty-one countries and the United States. Although as recently as five years ago this study could have reasonably excluded NATO, the unprecedented attention the organization has given to the Indo-Pacific, and China specifically, since 2019 makes it an increasingly relevant case-of-interest. The Taiwan-related rhetoric of NATO's long-serving Secretary-General Jens Stoltenberg – a former Norwegian prime minister – has been particularly striking.

Although neither the EU nor any of the three nation-states examined in this section possesses territory in East Asia,[10] each has played an important role in shaping the flexibility and effective meaning of the "One China" framework internationally. As with the three major Western Pacific U.S. allies examined in Section 3, upon recognizing the PRC during the Cold War, neither the UK (1950/1972), France (1964), West Germany (1972), nor the EU (1975) endorsed Beijing's claim of sovereignty over Taiwan. Importantly, all these entities adopted these positions and recognized Beijing before the United States did. Lastly, all these cases also demonstrate another core contention of this study: Regardless of official positions on "One China," how democratically elected leaders choose to operationalize their effective policies vis-à-vis Taiwan and the

---

[10] France has territories, 1.6 million citizens, and several thousand troops in the Indo-Pacific, though none in East Asia. The French territory closest to Taiwan – New Caledonia – is 4,200 miles away.

Taiwan Strait varies. (Given its unique status as a nongovernment organization and alliance without an official position on "One China," the NATO-specific analysis is limited to recent, unprecedented Taiwan-related statements from NATO and its leaders.)

4.1 The United Kingdom

4.1.1 The Origins and Post-1950 Evolution of the UK's Approach to Taiwan

In January 1950, just three months after the PRC's establishment, the UK government recognized the new communist regime headquartered in Beijing as "the de jure Government of China." London's reasons were manifold, and included its desires to protect its vast economic interests in China and to safeguard its colony in Hong Kong (Tsang 1994, 105–106). Given the UK's own concerns about Communism and its unique status as the sole additional cosigner – alongside the United States and ROC – of the wartime Cairo Declaration,[11] London's public break with Washington was significant. It also gave the UK the distinction of being the first major Western power and first U.S. treaty ally to recognize Mao's nascent communist regime. Given the UK's unique "first-mover" status, this case study focuses primarily on the origins and substance of London's position on Taiwan's status after recognizing the PRC.

Although it is common knowledge that in recognizing the PRC London broke with its wartime allies (the United States and ROC), less widely appreciated is that the UK government did so without recognizing the PRC claim of sovereignty over Taiwan. In fact, the UK Foreign Secretary's unilateral note conferring recognition on Beijing – there was no bilaterally negotiated communique – avoided even mentioning "Taiwan" (*New York Times* 1950). Furthermore, London's maintenance of a diplomatic consulate near Taipei angered China's leaders and severely damaged the nascent UK–PRC relationship. As a result, the UK and PRC would not reach a formal agreement to exchange chargés d'affaires until 1954, and they would not establish full ambassador-level diplomatic relations until 1972.

Whereas both the PRC and ROC have long sought to buttress their respective claims of sovereignty over Taiwan by citing the 1943 Cairo Declaration, the UK government's official position is that this wartime document was "merely a statement of intention ... [that] ... cannot by itself transfer sovereignty."

---

[11] The unilateral declaration by the three wartime allies stipulated that "all the territories Japan has stolen from the Chinese, such as Manchuria, Formosa, and The Pescadores, shall be restored to the Republic of China" (Cairo Declaration 1943).

As 1955 testimony in the House of Commons demonstrates, in London's official judgment:

> "The sovereignty [over Taiwan] was Japanese until 1952. The [San Francisco Peace] Treaty came into force, and at that time Formosa was being administered by the Chinese Nationalists, to whom it was entrusted in 1945, as a military occupation. In 1952 we did not recognise the Chinese Nationalists as representing the Chinese State. Therefore this military occupancy [after 1945] could not give them legal sovereignty nor, equally, could the Chinese People's Republic, which was not in occupation of Formosa, derive any rights from occupation of that territory." Accordingly, "Formosa and the Pescadores are therefore, in the view of Her Majesty's Government, territory the de jure sovereignty over which is uncertain or undetermined." (Hansard 1955a, b)

According to Michael Reilly, London's representative in Taipei from 2005 to 2009, after 1945 the UK government considered Taiwan to be "under military occupation by China," and "would not recognize that the government of China yet had a right to confer their nationality on the inhabitants of Taiwan" (Reilly 2020, 83). It considered Taiwan to be Japanese territory until 1952, at which point Japan renounced its title to Taiwan but – importantly – did not transfer it to either "China" (Bush 2004, 93). As Reilly summarizes London's official position then and now:

> Although [after recognizing the PRC in 1950] the UK no longer recognized the RoC as a state, nor did it recognize the PRC's claim to Taiwan. Its formal legal position was that the RoC government was the de facto government of the territories over which it exercised control but that de jure sovereignty over Taiwan remained undetermined, a position the British government continues to hold to this day, although in deference to Chinese sensitivities it is almost never stated. (Reilly 2020, 69–70)

During the foundational 1950–1958 period, Steve Tsang notes that British leaders did not consider continued recognition of the ROC regime – an issue distinct from whether Taiwan and the people living on it were part of a greater "China" – essential for achieving their more fundamental objective: keeping Taiwan out of CCP control. Indeed, to both Mao's and Chiang Kai-shek's dismay, the UK initially sought to keep "all options open for a future solution to the problem of Taiwan, ranging from independent statehood, a United Nations trusteeship, to a continuation of the existing Kuomintang government under Chiang" (Tsang 1994).

Nevertheless, as introduced in Section 2, Chiang's tight grip on power, his steadfast adherence to the KMT/ROC government's own version of the "one-China principle," and his stated desire to "reunify" China under the KMT banner made the prospect of Taiwan's "independence" from China and/or "self-determination" for the people in Taiwan nonstarters in Taipei. Eventually, British policy "drift[ed] towards a *de facto* two-China situation," with leaders prioritizing the cross-Strait status quo. Also contributing to this outcome were shifting geopolitics after the 1950–1953 Korean War (which saw British and Chinese troops fighting on opposing sides), London's desire to maintain positive ties with its U.S. ally, and Chiang's effective abandonment in 1958 of his goal to retake the Chinese mainland by force (Tsang 1994).

By the early 1970s, however, international political winds had shifted again. After PRC representatives were admitted into the UN (1971) and Nixon concluded his historic 1972 visit to China, London negotiated a bilateral communique with Beijing in which it agreed to remove its "official representation in Taiwan." In return, Beijing allowed an exchange of ambassadors. Even so, UK leaders still refused to endorse the PRC's claim of sovereignty over Taiwan: In the March 1972 joint communique London adopted a version of the Canadian formula that merely "acknowledges *the position of the Chinese government* that Taiwan is a province of the [PRC]" (emphasis added). (Hansard 1972) It avoids explicitly stating the UK's own official position: that Taiwan's status is undetermined.

Especially as a first mover, close U.S. treaty ally, and signatory of the Cairo Declaration, the UK's choices before and after 1950 had profound consequences for Taiwan. If the UK had actually endorsed the PRC's sovereignty claim in 1950 or 1972, perhaps due to concerns about Hong Kong or its extensive and growing economic interests in China, it almost certainly would have severely limited options for the United States and its other allies during their own normalization negotiations with Beijing – to say nothing of the significant implications for the people in Taiwan. But British leaders chose not to do so.

4.1.2 The Contemporary Situation

Fifty years after 1972, the UK and Taiwan maintain fruitful, if "unofficial," ties centered on de facto representative offices, parliamentary exchanges, and trade, inter alia. London's official position on Taiwan's status remains unchanged since the 1950s. Nevertheless, reflecting trends that manifest across most U.S. ally cases, practical bilateral engagement has deepened – especially after the 1980s. Over the past decade, in particular, the UK government and Parliament have both become increasingly outspoken about Taiwan and cross-Strait peace and stability.

Since the late 1980s, London and Taipei have gradually expanded de facto ties, including upgrading unofficial representation in their respective capitals. In

1993, London renamed its "Anglo-Taiwan Trade Committee," which began issuing visas in June 1989, as "the British Trade and Cultural Office." The latter was further upgraded and renamed "British Office Taipei" in 2015. The British-Taiwanese All-Party Parliamentary Group, established in 1976, has expanded to roughly 140 members. Recent years have witnessed an uptick in high-level visits: for example, over the past decade the UK's Lord Speaker and members of the House of Commons Foreign Affairs Committee have visited Taiwan and the President of Taiwan's Legislative Yuan has visited the UK (TRO UK 2024). Meanwhile, the UK trade minister met with President Tsai in Taipei in 2022, while Taiwan's Digital Minister visited London in June 2023 and met with Britain's security minister (*Reuters* 2023e).

Regarding support for Taiwan's international space and cross-Strait peace and stability today, UK expressions of interest and concern are increasingly mainstream and appear basically aligned with the United States and other major allies. As an FCDO Minister noted in 2020, the UK and Taiwan have "a strong unofficial relationship based on dynamic commercial, educational and cultural ties," adding that "We regularly lobby in favour of Taiwan's participation in international organisations where statehood is not a prerequisite, and we make clear our concerns about any activity that risks destabilising the cross-strait status quo" (UK Parliament 2020).

Since that 2020 statement, the UK has championed multilateral statements of support, most notably when – as G7 host in 2021 – it drafted the first foreign minister communique to "support Taiwan's meaningful participation" in the World Health Assembly, and the first summit communique to reference the Taiwan Strait and call for "peaceful resolution of cross-Strait issues" (G7 2021a, b). London has also signed on to all subsequent, more forward-leaning G7 statements, and even released bilateral statements with other U.S. allies and partners, such as the 2023 Australia-UK 2+2 joint statement (DFAT 2023a).

Unsurprisingly, the UK remains deliberately ambiguous regarding how it would respond to a cross-Strait contingency. Nevertheless, London has reportedly approved an increase of defense-related exports to Taiwan – at least $200 million worth in the first nine months of 2022, more than the previous six years combined (*Reuters* 2023d). Taiwan's largest military development program, its indigenous submarine project, reportedly relies on technology sourced from "at least seven countries," including the UK (*Reuters* 2021b). London also sent military vessels through the Taiwan Strait in 2019 and 2021, with the latter, involving the frigate HMS *Richmond*, marking the first transit by a UK warship since 2008 (AFP 2021).

Since 2022, the year of both Russia's full-scale invasion of Ukraine and massive PLA exercises around Taiwan in response to Pelosi's visit to Taipei,

British concerns have been repeatedly expressed at the highest and most official levels. For example, in November 2022 Prime Minister Rishi Sunak stated that "there should be no unilateral change to the status and there should be a peaceful resolution," adding, vaguely, "We stand ready to support Taiwan as we do in standing up to Chinese aggression" (*The Guardian* 2022b). Five months later, the UK's 2023 Integrated Review of Security, Defence, Development and Foreign Policy mentioned Taiwan for the first time. In the foreword, Sunak characterized the war in Ukraine and China's actions in the South China Sea and Taiwan Strait as "threatening to create a world defined by danger, disorder and division – and an international order more favourable to authoritarianism." The document also reiterated Britain's stance: "The UK's long-standing position remains that the Taiwan issue should be settled peacefully by people on both sides of the Taiwan Strait through dialogue, and not through any unilateral attempts to change the status quo" (HM Government 2023).

4.2 France

4.2.1 The Origins and Post-1964 Evolution of France's Approach to Taiwan

In 1964, France became both the first major U.S. ally to recognize Beijing after North Korea's PRC-backed 1950 invasion of South Korea and the first major Western power with which the PRC exchanged ambassadors, thereby establishing full diplomatic relations. Beyond President Charles de Gaulle's reported desire to "recognize the world as it is," French Gaullists also saw this conspicuous break with Washington as demonstrating Paris' independence from America and a shift of international politics beyond the "East-West divide." On the one hand, France's move predictably infuriated the administration of U.S. President Lyndon Johnson. On the other hand, and of particular relevance for this study, Nixon would later credit de Gaulle for influencing his decision to move the United States toward recognizing Beijing. In marking the sixtieth anniversary in 2024, Xi Jinping judged de Gaulle's move "a major event in the history of international relations" (*Le Monde* 2024). It was, and therefore deserves significant consideration for the terms under which it was carried out.

The fact that de Gaulle's government refused to endorse the PRC's claim to Taiwan despite his eagerness to demonstrate independence from Washington makes clear that Paris had its own reasons for doing so. According to a contemporaneous UK assessment, de Gaulle wished to avoid "go[ing] against the principle of self-determination by saying that Formosa was part of China without any indication of the wishes of the Formosa population." Accordingly, before his departure to negotiate with Beijing, French Prime Minister Edgar

Faure was reportedly ordered not to make any commitment regarding the future status of Taiwan (Shin 2001, 127). France sought to maintain some official link to Taipei (such as a consulate, like the UK) after normalization, and to explore possibilities for a "two China" policy (Cabestan 2001, 2). On the eve of France officially recognizing the PRC, de Gaulle even reportedly told Chiang Kai-shek that if the ROC leader would "declare the ROC a new state limiting its territory to the island of Taiwan, France would recognize the new State and the ROC as its legitimate government." Fatefully, Chiang refused (Chiang 2017, 137). Chiang's staunch nationalism and adherence to the ROC's version of the "one-China principle" made dual recognition anathema.

Nevertheless, in the 1964 France–PRC communique Paris successfully parried Beijing's demands to explicitly recognize the PRC "as the sole legal government of China" and to break off diplomatic relations with the ROC. The short statement conspicuously lacked any reference to "Taiwan" or even "One China." Ultimately, it was the ROC government – despite last-minute efforts by Washington to persuade Chiang otherwise – that unilaterally severed diplomatic ties with France. As a result, for a short time France had diplomatic ties with both "Chinas" (Martin 2008, 78) To prevent later U.S. allies from concluding from France's experience that Beijing would accept "two Chinas" or "one China, one Taiwan," however, the PRC launched a propaganda campaign asserting that it would never again make similar concessions (Fukuda 2012). Six years later, Ottawa would creatively square the circle through its path-breaking "Canadian Formula" (see Section 2), which mentioned "One China" and Taiwan explicitly but nevertheless avoided endorsing Beijing's sovereignty claim.

As in other cases, how France–Taiwan unofficial relations would be operationalized in practice after Paris recognized Beijing would be left up to political leaders to decide. Despite the fact that France's 1964 communique with Beijing did not even mention "Taiwan" or "One China," the "unofficial" relationship between Paris and Taipei for many years following was hardly robust. After 1964, Taiwan was not a priority; French interests in Taipei were represented only by "a handful of businesspeople with the aloof assistance of the French consulate in Hong Kong" (Cabestan 2001, 3–4).

By the 1980s, however, and against the backdrop of vastly changed political circumstances, a different generation of French officials emerged to lead Europe in pursuing unprecedented engagement with Taiwan – at times even moving ahead of Washington. As Shin sums up the decade, "the French government not only broke the 'no-contact-with-Taiwan' policy but also reinterpreted the meaning of "One China" (2001, 139). In 1978 and 1980, Paris established in Taipei French associations for economic development and culture and science, respectively (MOFA(ROC) 2022) Several years later, France became the first European country not recognizing the ROC to issue visas via its office in Taipei. (Other European representative offices soon followed). Within a year, the rank of the Association's head of office was upgraded to a retired ambassador (Mengin 2002, 145–46). The 1989–1993 period saw a further deepening of ties as the Cold War ended in Europe, Taiwan's democratization and economic growth accelerated, and France–PRC relations worsened in the wake of Beijing's brutal crackdown on protesters in June 1989 – on which France took a very critical public stand. In Shin's words, "deterioration in PRC–France relations ... open[ed] up breathing space for ROC-France relations" (2001, 145).

In aggregate, Paris' moves after 1989 exploded the myths that France–Taiwan relations were strictly economic and cultural and that there were nonnegotiable bounds on bilateral engagement locked in after Paris recognized Beijing. In July 1989, just one month after Tiananmen Square, ROC Foreign Minister Lien Chan was invited to Paris by the French Senate's president to mark the 200th anniversary of the French Revolution. The French government soon allowed visits from multiple ROC ministers, including Taiwan's minister of transportation in 1990 (Shin 2001, 145–7). Meanwhile, Paris upgraded France's "cultural" office to the status of "French Institute in Taipei" (FIT;[12] mirroring AIT) with every consular function, and even appointed as its new director an ambassador-rank diplomat "who had taken early retirement." Other European countries, including the UK and Germany, soon followed France's lead and began appointing foreign ministry personnel to Taipei (Cabestan 2001, 10–11; Mengin 2002, 145–6; Shin 2001 138–9, 147).

In another precedent-setting step, in January 1991 France became the first government having diplomatic relations with the PRC to send a cabinet minister to Taiwan. Yet again, other European governments followed France's lead. Over the next thirty months, more than twenty European cabinet members visited Taipei. In sending a cabinet minister to Taiwan, France was nearly two years ahead of the U.S. government, which did not send its first Cabinet-level representative until November 1992 (Mengin 2002, 145–6).

The trend continued: In 1993, Paris further upgraded the FIT director post to be filled by a career diplomat on "temporary secondment" (Mengin 2002, 145–46) and split the "China Desk" in France's foreign ministry to allow a diplomat to focus on Taiwan. French and Taiwanese ministers also began to sign high-level

---

[12] Paris would later change the official French name from "Institut" to "Bureau" (office) to avoid confusion with the similarly named "Institut Français" – which promotes French culture overseas.

joint legal declarations. Several secret visits by high-ranking military officials also reportedly occurred (Cabestan 2001, 5–11).

Belying the contemporary myth that only the United States has dared to sell major military platforms to Taipei, during this period Paris even approved sales to Taiwan of six naval frigates (1991) and sixty fighter jets (1992). These sales further demonstrated Paris' strikingly flexible interpretation of the 1964 France–PRC communique and the politically determined bounds of the "One China" framework. According to Cabestan, this "military co-operation" was driven by Tiananmen, Taiwan's democratization, and the French defense industry's need for new markets following the Soviet Union's collapse (Cabestan 2001, 5–6).

It was ultimately these arms sales that proved too much for Beijing, which responded by ordering France to close its Guangzhou consulate and banned French companies from participating in a major subway project. (Probably not coincidentally, the subway contract was awarded to a German company after the German chancellor vetoed a proposed sale of German warships to Taiwan (*New York Times* 1994).)

To control the damage, in 1994 a new French government that coveted China's vast and growing market potential made a striking political concession to Beijing. It negotiated a new bilateral communique with Beijing that "recogniz[ed]" Taiwan as part of "Chinese territory" (*une partie intégrante du territoire chinois*). The new communique also committed Paris "not to authorize any French enterprises to participate in the arming of Taiwan" (Ministère des Affaires étrangères 1994). Although in using wording roughly consistent with the ruling KMT's own view on "One China" France's new leaders stopped short of endorsing Beijing's view that Taiwan is part *of the PRC*, the new language appeared to go meaningfully beyond both the literal text and original intent of the 1964 normalization communique, as well as the intentionally vague "Canadian Formula" adopted by the United States and most U.S. democratic allies after 1970. The fundamentally political nature of Paris' efforts to improve relations with Beijing and curtail arms sales in response to severe blowback was clear. Foreign Minister Alain Juppé (1993–1995) publicly defended the shift as based on a "pragmatic" long-term assessment of national interests considering China's international economic and political importance (Juppé 1993).

Though France's 1994 political statement departed from its 1964 position on "One China" and effectively ended French willingness to sell major weapons platforms to Taiwan, Paris continued to deepen its practical engagement with Taiwan. Within a year France agreed to upgrade the ROC's presence in Paris, which was newly named the "Taipei Representative Office in France" (Cabestan 2001, 5–11). France also again upgraded the FIT director post, which thenceforth was filled by an ambassador-level career diplomat, who also oversaw an increasingly large staff (Mengin 2002, 145–46). In short, in exchange for a high-profile and largely *political* concession in 1994, Beijing effectively accepted a de facto new status quo: incrementally deeper France–Taiwan relations, all under a politically tolerable veneer of unofficiality.

As further evidence of the role of political interpretation defining practical policy bounds, even France's official interpretation of the ambiguously worded 1994 pledge on "arming of Taiwan" was at odds with Beijing's. Paris continued to allow a few additional (if smaller) deals and military and technical cooperation, including Taiwanese and French pilots on each other's soil. Juppé and his defense counterpart even unilaterally asserted that France had committed only to show "reserve" (*retenue*) and not to sell "offensive weapons" – suggesting that U.S.-style "defensive" arms sales were still theoretically allowable (Cabestan 2001, 13–15; Mengin 2002, 147). Thus, although France has not again sold new weapons platforms on the scale of 1991–1992, in unilaterally asserting this interpretation its leaders effectively carved out space to potentially allow them in the future. In other words, whether such sales occur was to be based not on legal or other commitment, but on political leaders' judgment – one which will inevitably take into consideration, but not necessarily be beholden to, Beijing's likely response.

4.2.2 The Contemporary Situation

More recent developments raise additional questions about the practical long-term significance of the 1994 France-PRC communique (which "recognized" Taiwan as part of "Chinese territory"). On the one hand, in the years following joint statements explicitly referenced Taiwan, and some French leaders occasionally reiterated the 1994 communique's language on "One China," such as when the Sarkozy government referenced it in a statement opposing DPP President Chen Shui-bian's (2000–2008) pursuit of a referendum on UN membership (*Reuters* 2007).

On the other hand, under President Emmanuel Macron (2017–) the French government may be attempting to quietly distance Paris from its predecessors' rhetorical concessions to Beijing. For starters, recent France–PRC joint statements have stopped mentioning "Taiwan" altogether. Furthermore, when asserting Paris' "constant" "one China policy" France's past three foreign ministers have avoided referencing the 1994 communique. Instead, they refer to the 1964 communique, which said nothing about Taiwan. Additionally, they have repeatedly emphasized constructive cross-Strait dialogue, opposed unilateral changes to the status quo, and expressed support for Taiwan's participation in international organizations (e.g., Drian 2021; *Libération* 2022; Ministère de l'Europe et des Affaires étrangères 2023).

This apparent shift occurs alongside what appear to be the Macron government's more recent efforts to firmly align France's position and policy with those of the EU, the United States, and other U.S. allies, even as Macron has also expressed concern about being seen as following the United States and/or risking a Chinese overreaction. In 2023, Macron asserted at The Hague that "The French and European position on Taiwan is the same one. We're in favour of the status quo. This policy is constant and hasn't changed," adding, "It's the One-China policy and a Pacific resolution of the situation. That's what I said in my one-to-one meeting with Xi Jinping, that's what was said everywhere, we haven't changed" (*Reuters* 2023b). The French Office in Taipei asserted that "France's position on Taiwan is constant," while conspicuously avoiding a reference to the 1994 communique. Instead, it flagged various bilateral and multilateral statements, including from the G7, the EU's High Representative, the EU Indo-Pacific strategy, and bilateral declarations with the United States, Australia, and the UK (Bureau Français de Taipei 2023). All these statements also avoid mentioning the sovereignty question or whether Taiwan belongs to "Chinese territory."

Meanwhile, France's Senate and National Assembly also appear eager to demonstrate their own support for Taiwan's international space and efforts to deepen ties with Taiwan. For example, in 2021 both bodies (including the Senate by a striking margin of 304 to 0) passed resolutions supporting Taiwan's participation in international organizations such as the UN Framework Convention on Climate Change, Interpol, and the World Health Assembly (*RFI* 2021). That year, over the repeated objections of the PRC embassy in France, which alleged such visits "clearly violate the one-China principle," multiple delegations of French senators and National Assembly members representing different parliamentary groups also visited Taiwan and met with President Tsai (e.g., *France 24* 2021).

Regarding cross-Strait frictions, especially since the Pelosi visit France has become remarkably assertive and frank. In a 2022 interview, France's commander of Armed Forces in the Asia-Pacific identified France's naval transits through the Taiwan Strait as a reaction to the PRC's "completely wrong" assertions that it has "sovereign rights" over the "international strait" (*Taipei Times* 2022). The November 2022 National Strategic Review specifically highlighted China's "increasingly assertive strategy, including on the military front … particularly with regard to the status quo in the Taiwan Strait" ("National Strategic Review 2022" 2022). That year, France also became the first European country to mention Taiwan and the Taiwan Strait in its Indo-Pacific strategy (MEFA 2022). Lastly, in 2023 France called for peaceful resolution and no unilateral changes to the status quo in multilateral G7 statements and bilateral statements with fellow U.S. allies Australia and Japan. The former additionally committed Paris to "support Taiwan's meaningful participation in the work of international organisations, where statehood is not a prerequisite" and to "deepening relations with Taiwan" (Gaimushō 2023b; MEFA 2023).

As further indication of French efforts, despite the 1994 communique, to present a united front with the EU, the United States, and other U.S. allies, at a major July 2023 international forum Macron's diplomatic advisor Emmanuel Bonne stated that "the key components of our China policy, or Taiwan policy, are exactly the same as the US administration." He specifically noted a "One China policy" and the desire for a "peaceful solution." He also stated that France conducts Taiwan Strait transits "every year" and that France would "be with [the U.S.] in case of crisis," adding that "in terms of principles, solidarity, and what needs to be done, we are exactly on the same page, and what matters most . . . is to deter China from taking action." He further revealed that during Macron's meeting with Xi the French president conveyed that if China acted, "that will have a big price [and . . .] will force us to go for massive sanctions etcetera and probably much more" (Aspen Institute 2023).

In short, beyond the abstract question of its official position on "One China," Paris' deepening engagement with and regarding Taiwan and the Taiwan Strait is, in practical terms, vastly different today than it was in 1964. As successive governments' observable shifts on arms sales and variable willingness to reference the 1994 communique demonstrate, it has ebbed and flowed in the interim. Developments over the past thirty years make clear that the constraining power of past communiques is subjectively – and politically – determined.

4.3 Germany

4.3.1 The Origins and Post-1972 Evolution of Germany's Approach to Taiwan

The Federal Republic of Germany (FRG; aka "West Germany" until German unification in 1990) was born after World War II with no preexisting diplomatic relationship with either the ROC or PRC. Given Germany's own Cold War–era division, FRG leaders originally opted not to recognize either "China." In 1972, however, after PRC representatives had already been granted "China's" UN seat and Nixon visited China, they decided to recognize Beijing.

Even so, the October 1972 FRG–PRC communique conspicuously made no mention of "Taiwan." This fact gave Bonn the distinction of being the only major U.S. ally after France (1964) to avoid any reference to Taiwan or "One China" in a bilateral normalization communique. The reason, however, was less about

Taiwan than the fact that Germany itself was divided. Both Beijing and Bonn wished to avoid taking a position on the other's division (Mengin 1997, 241).

Although the 1972 communique did not articulate Germany's position on the sovereignty question, especially after 1990 Beijing used the PRC's support for German unification to pressure Berlin to support China's "reunification" with Taiwan. With 1972 as the baseline, the ambiguity of Germany's official position declined over time. Eventually, it adopted a public position like Paris' in the 1994 France–PRC communique: Berlin has identified Taiwan as part of "China." Nevertheless, it avoids endorsing *the PRC's* claim of sovereignty over Taiwan.

One example is the 2004 joint statement released during PRC Premier Wen Jiabao's visit to Berlin to meet Chancellor Gerhard Schroeder (1998–2005). Consistent with a recurring theme of this study – that positions and policies vis-à-vis "One China" are politically contingent – this statement was released at a moment of great optimism in Germany about China's surging market potential, severe tensions between the Schroeder government and its U.S. ally over the Iraq War, and deepening concerns in Berlin about DPP President Chen Shui-bian's flirtations with a possible declaration of de jure independence. Schroeder himself was also widely considered a relatively pro-China politician; for example, around this time he also famously pressed the EU to lift the arms embargo imposed after Beijing's bloody crackdown on pro-democracy protesters in 1989 (*Reuters* 2018).

During Wen's 2004 visit, Schroeder agreed to a 1,400-word "joint declaration" that included three sentences related to "One China." It stated that Germany's "federal government" will "support peaceful reunification of China" (friedliche Wiedervereinigung Chinas unterstützt) and "opposes the 'independence' of Taiwan" ('Unabhängigkeit' von Taiwan). It also opposed "all steps aimed at escalating tensions [Verschärfung der Spannungen] in the Taiwan Strait" (China.org.cn 2004). Taken at face value, the first two positions evinced meaningful differences with those of the United States and several other key U.S. allies, which avoid expressing preferences about the cross-Strait dispute's ultimate outcome. A contemporaneous newspaper article judged that the statement meant the German government was "backing China's position on the Taiwan question more clearly than ever before" (*Der Spiegel* 2004).

Nevertheless, Berlin's official position on "One China" still differs from Beijing's "one-China principle." At a 2019 hearing in response to a petition demanding that the Federal Government "establish full diplomatic relations with the Republic of China (Taiwan)," Petra Sigmund, then the Foreign Office's Director-General for Asia and the Pacific, explained that Germany "recognizes only the [PRC] as the only sovereign state in China" (nur die Volksrepublik China als einzigen souveränen Staat in China an), adding that "for us, Taiwan is part of China" (für uns ist Taiwan ein Teil Chinas). Notably, however, according to contemporaneous media reports she reportedly implied that "China" does not necessarily refer to the PRC. Sigmund stated matter-of-factly why Germany sticks to its ambiguous "One China" policy, noting that abandoning it "would seriously damage German-Chinese relations" (schwerwiegend beschädigen) and "That is not in our interest" (Das liegt nicht in unserem Interesse) (Deutscher Bundestag 2019; *DW* 2019). Two legal scholars in Germany summed up Sigmund's response as based partially on a judgment that the ROC government's own official position is that it is not "a separate independent state" but part of "one 'China'" (Sinha and Talmon 2019).

Regardless, what consequence Berlin's official "One China" position has for official rhetoric and policy toward Taiwan is far from clear-cut. For instance, in her 2019 testimony Sigmund highlighted positions on more practical matters clearly aligned with the United States and others. For example, she emphasized that the German government "wants to maintain the status quo of our relations with Taiwan without any conditions and . . . rejects any unilateral change to the status quo," adding that it regularly tells Beijing "that unification between the People's Republic of China and Taiwan can only take place peacefully and on the basis of a dialogue characterized by mutual respect." She further noted exchanges with Taiwan in many areas "beneath the level of diplomatic relations through the relevant specialist departments up to the ministerial level," adding that "we do not always make it public when such contacts happen." Notably, Sigmund also called for "expanding" the bilateral relationship "further" and stated that Berlin is "strongly committed to enabling Taiwan to participate meaningfully in international organizations" where appropriate. She continued, "We actively promote the continuation of these contacts with Taiwan and, even if this is not always seen favorably by Beijing, we confidently advocate this position because it reflects the current status quo with Taiwan" (Deutscher Bundestag 2019).

Germany's push to "expand" the bilateral relationship is now decades old. Indeed, especially after 1989 Germany's efforts to deepen practical economic, political, and de facto diplomatic ties with Taiwan paralleled similar trends in the United States, France, and other major U.S. allies. Government officials at the central and federal state levels began to travel to Taiwan. In 1992, Germany's economic minister became the first to visit Taipei. In 2000, the German government established the "German Institute Taipei (GIT)," which took over consular duties from what had been called the German Trade Office and functioned "as the unofficial representation of the FRG in Taiwan" (Schubert 2001, 9–10). Importantly, the newly upgraded Institute's diplomatic staff were thenceforth considered "on duty," no longer "on leave" (Mengin 2002, 145). In recent years, the Office has been headed by a career diplomat of "director general" rank (Sinha and Talmon 2019).

Despite the post-1990s trend of incrementally deepening ties with Taiwan, some important qualifiers are also necessary. First, Berlin has placed stricter constraints than some other U.S. allies on the level of official exchanges – even publicly and explicitly forbidding officials in seven high-ranking positions from engaging their counterparts in Taiwan (e.g., *Taiwanreporter* 2018). Second, the trend has not always been unidirectional. For example, although some German cabinet members were authorized to visit Taipei beginning in the early 1990s, no such visits occurred between 1998 and 2022. This period overlapped almost entirely with the Schroeder and Merkel administrations. Perhaps not coincidentally, this was also a period during which German exports to China increased 19-fold (World Bank 2024).

Third, as in other cases, German leaders have granted different policy domains differing political significance. For Berlin, security engagement with Taiwan has always been particularly controversial. The aforementioned aborted early 1990s arms sale – around the time Paris was considering (and ultimately approved) frigate and fighter jet sales to Taipei – is a case in point. As Schubert summarizes: in the early 1990s, Taiwan unsuccessfully lobbied the German government to permit the construction and sale of ten submarines and ten frigates. Although several German federal state governments supported the deal, the Federal Security Council rejected it in 1993 because "Taiwan was considered a zone of military insecurity to which no German 'dual use'-technology could be exported by law." In addition, "Foreign Minister Klaus Kinkel unequivocally ruled out at various occasions the selling of weapons to Taiwan in 1992." Notably, this was not a formal or across-the-board ban, since subsequent reports revealed that the government agreed to the reexport of German missile components from the United States to Taiwan, and four German minesweepers were observed in Taiwan in 1992 (Schubert 2001, 8–9). More recently, the German Parliament's Defense Committee chair has stated that Berlin will not provide weapons to Taiwan (*Reuters* 2023a). Similar to Japan, it is difficult to parse to what extent this self-imposed ban reflects concerns about arms sales *to Taiwan* rather than general reluctance to export arms to any "zone of military insecurity."

4.3.2 The Contemporary Situation

Despite some subtle apparent daylight between Germany's official position on "One China" and that of the United States and some other allies, the extent and nature of Berlin's engagement with and official rhetoric regarding Taiwan and the Taiwan Strait have shifted notably toward greater alignment since late 2021.

That this shift has occurred largely after the resignation of the long-serving and powerful Chancellor Merkel (2005–2021) makes Germany yet another case demonstrating the political contingency of major U.S. allies' approaches to Taiwan in practice.

The tripartite coalition (Social Democrats, Free Democrats, and Greens) that took power after Merkel stepped down promptly became more forward-leaning on Taiwan. Its December 2021 Coalition Agreement was the first ever to refer to "Taiwan" and "the Taiwan Strait," to insist that "any change in the status quo in the Taiwan Strait can only occur peacefully and by mutual consent," and to "support democratic Taiwan's substantive participation in international organizations" (Bundesregierung 2021). This was followed by several other remarkable "firsts" under the new government. A particularly high-profile example was Germany's September 2022 progress report on the implementation of its Indo-Pacific Policy Guidelines. This document referred to Taiwan as a "partner," expressed support for "issue-specific engagement by democratic Taiwan in international organisations," and stated that "the status quo in the Taiwan Strait can only be changed by peaceful means and by mutual agreement." It also clearly stipulated a national interest in such an outcome, noting, "Military escalation would also affect German and European interests" (Federal Government 2022). Two months later, Germany's chancellor openly discussed Taiwan in Beijing, noting that one "expectation" of Germany's "One China" policy is that changes to the status quo must be "by mutual agreement" (Bundesregierung 2022).

This trend of greater outspokenness continued in 2023 and 2024. In March 2023, Germany's coalition government became the first since 1997 to send a cabinet minister (Minister of Education and Research) to Taiwan. (Not coincidentally, both the 1997 visit and the 2023 visit involved a Cabinet member from the Free Democratic Party, a founding member of Liberal International – a world federation of liberal political parties, of which Taiwan's ruling DPP is also a member.) The following month, Germany's foreign minister publicly stated in Beijing that neither Germany nor the EU can "be indifferent to the tensions in the Taiwan Strait," adding that "free access" is in Germany's economic interest (*Politico* 2023). Over the summer, Germany's chancellor told the PRC's premier that "We firmly reject all unilateral attempts to change the status quo in the East and South China Seas by force or coercion. This is especially true for Taiwan" (*Reuters* 2023c). Meanwhile, a remarkable July saw the first meeting of Germany's and Taiwan's justice ministers (*Focus Taiwan* 2023) and the release of Germany's first-ever China strategy. It mentioned Taiwan or the Taiwan Strait twelve times and expressed concern about "Chinese disinformation campaigns" (FRG 2023). Lastly, in September 2024, two German naval ships transited the Taiwan Strait for the first time since 2002. They were backed up by statements from Germany's chancellor and defense minister that the Strait is "international waters" (*Naval News* 2024).

The coalition government has on at least one occasion gone out of its way to publicly emphasize the distinction between Beijing's "one-China principle" and Germany's "one China" policy. During a strikingly frank December 2022 speech, Martin Thümmel, Germany's deputy-director general for Asia, directly rejected Beijing's efforts to misleadingly conflate its "one-China principle" with Berlin's "One China" policy, and to define for Germany what actions are or are not within bounds. In his words: "We [Germany] have our One China policy [and while maintaining its "basic pillars" . . .] it is us who have devised this policy and *it is us who interpret this policy – no one else*." He additionally criticized Beijing's "very selective interpretation" of UN 2758, which had done "nothing more" than "establish the PRC as the sole representative of China in the UN," and its efforts to raise doubts about whether the Taiwan Strait is "international waters." Thümmel went on to blame Beijing for the "turn for the worse" in cross-Strait relations and for "trying to isolate Taiwan internationally and prevent its participation . . . in international organizations and other frameworks." Paralleling language from the United States and some other major U.S. allies, he additionally stated that "Taiwan is far more than just an economic or cultural partner. It is a value partner and . . . a leading or maybe the leading democracy in Asia," and called for efforts to "counter" Beijing's "economic coercion." He closed by noting that "The federal government will continue to support and seek its own contacts and support contacts by others and to have a much more meaningful and long-lasting relationship with Taiwan on all levels" (Thümmel 2022).

A Foreign Office official's statement several months earlier, in the immediate wake of the PLA's large-scale August 2022 exercises around Taiwan, further highlighted Germany's alignment with the United States and other allies, stating,

> Just like the U.S., we have long pursued a one-China policy, and we recognize the People's Republic of China as the only sovereign state in China . . . At the same time, Germany has long maintained close relations with Taiwan as part of our One China policy, particularly in the areas of business, culture, education, science and research. As a consolidated democracy with high human rights standards, Taiwan is a value partner and also an important economic partner for Germany. Our view is that a change in the status quo in the Taiwan Strait can only take place peacefully and by mutual consent of all parties involved and that such visits should not be used as an occasion for

military threatening gestures and the use of economic means of coercion. We are working with our international partners to contribute to de-escalation in the Taiwan Strait. (Auswärtiges Amt 2022)

The German case provides additional support for a core theme of this study: that the contours of "acceptable" rhetoric and policy vis-à-vis Taiwan and the Taiwan Strait under U.S. allies' "One China" policies are – to paraphrase the Foreign Office official quoted earlier – up to their political leaders to devise and interpret; and "no one else." Recent developments post-Merkel represent a striking shift in tone and, arguably, a subtle shift in practical policy and effort. A clear implication is closer alignment with the United States, EU, and other democratic partners of Taiwan. And all this despite no change in decades to Germany's official position on "One China," which leans closer to Beijing's preferences than those of the United States, UK, or several other major U.S. democratic treaty allies. Even so, what matters most is its distinction with Beijing's one-China principle and how it has been variably politically interpreted (and reinterpreted) in Berlin over the past half-century.

4.4 The European Union

Given the EU's unique origins, its long-standing reputation as a primarily economic actor, and China's status as its top trading partner, the extent to which its main decision-making institutions – especially the European Commission and Parliament – have emerged recently as a major force in Europe mainstreaming more outspoken rhetoric and increasing engagement with Taiwan among its twenty-seven member states is striking. This development is especially remarkable given the EU's complex foreign policymaking process and norms of consensus among its diverse member states, which scholars generally consider to make "coherent common positions" difficult, especially on sensitive or complicated topics (Brown 2022).

4.4.1 The Origins and Post-1975 Evolution of the EU's Approach to Taiwan

The modern EU ("Brussels") did not exist before 1992. Accordingly, it was its predecessor – the European Economic Community – that in 1975 established diplomatic relations with the PRC. This decision followed the first official visit to China by the Vice-President of the European Commission (EC), a visit during which Beijing – in Zhang Xiaotong's words – demanded that the VP "formally and publicly declare that Taiwan was geographically an integral part of China" (Zhang 2014). This PRC pressure campaign failed, however. As the VP later reported to the European Parliament (EP), "recognition of states did not come within the responsibility of the Community" and he was "able to satisfy" Beijing with a vague, conspicuously present-tense, matter-of-fact statement that "the Community does not entertain any official relations with Taiwan or have any agreements with it" (Soames 1975).

Neither then nor since has Brussels adopted a position endorsing Beijing's claim that Taiwan is part of PRC territory. Nor has it agreed to any statement which would preclude certain policy options regarding the future treatment of Taiwan.

After the EU gained the authority to recognize states in the 1990s, its leaders continued to avoid explicitly endorsing Beijing's sovereignty claim. For example, EU–China summit statements going back at least to the early 2000s contain either vague, unilateral assertions of "continued adherence to the one China policy" and "hope for a peaceful resolution of the Taiwan question through constructive dialogue," or no such references at all (e.g., MFA(PRC) 2004). At least as early as its 2006 China strategy, the EC emphasized that "The EU has a significant stake in the maintenance of cross-straits peace and stability" and, "on the basis of its One China Policy," pledged "to take an active interest, and to make its views known to both sides." It emphasized the EU's "opposition to any measure which would amount to a unilateral change of the status quo; strong opposition to the use of force; encouragement for pragmatic solutions and confidence building measures; support for dialogue between all parties; and, continuing strong economic and trade links with Taiwan" (European Commission 2006).

Although because they require EU member state approval EC or Council proclamations and actions can be considered more authoritative than those of the EP, the EP has also played an important role encouraging EU engagement with and on issues related to Taiwan and the Taiwan Strait. In 1995, it condemned Beijing's military exercises before Taiwan's first direct presidential election and passed a resolution urging the PRC to abandon the threat of force. It has also supported Taiwan's international space and Europe's bilateral engagement with Taipei, including a call around the same time to improve Taiwan's representation in international organizations. And in 2001 it called for the EC to set up an EU-level representative office in Taiwan (Mengin 2002, 153). The EU office in Taiwan began operation two years later. Now named the "European Economic and Trade Office," its own website notably refers to it as "the *official* representation of the European Union in Taiwan" (emphasis added) and reveals that – despite its name – it has a political section (EEAS 2021b).

The EU has also been outspoken in support of Taiwan's democracy. A 2008 declaration on cross-Strait relations by the EU presidency "on behalf of the European Union" welcomed Taiwan's presidential election, expressed "its support for Taiwan's democratic values," vaguely "reiterate[d] its One China policy and its firm support for a peaceful resolution of the Taiwan question," and stated that it "will continue to support Taiwan's practical participation in specialized multilateral fora where statehood is not a requirement" (Slovenian Presidency of the EU 2008). EU Council conclusions have similarly avoided endorsing Beijing's claim to Taiwan, preferring instead to vaguely reference the EU's "One China" policy.

In its 2016 China strategy, the EC again "confirm[ed] its 'One China' policy" – without stating what it is. In language more forward-leaning than even most major U.S. allies at the time, it included a full paragraph on Taiwan expressing the EC's "commitment to continuing to develop [EU] relations with Taiwan and to supporting the shared values underpinning its system of governance," "support [for] the constructive development of cross-Strait relations as part of keeping the Asia-Pacific region at peace," "us[ing] every available channel to encourage initiatives aimed at promoting dialogue, co-operation and confidence-building between the two sides of the Taiwan Strait," and "promot[ing] practical solutions regarding Taiwan's participation in international frameworks, wherever this is consistent with the EU's 'One China' policy and the EU's policy objectives" (European Commission 2016).

Simply put, while repeatedly reaffirming its (vague) "One China" policy, the EU has conspicuously avoided endorsing Beijing's claim that Taiwan is part of the PRC. (Further evincing the lack of a clear position on Taiwan's status, the EC's 1994 Asia strategy even referred to Taiwan as a "country" multiple times (European Commission 1994).) Regardless of the EU's official position on "One China," the long-term trend has been for the EU to gradually deepen its effective engagement with Taiwan, support Taiwan's international space, and articulate support for Taiwan's democracy and the importance of peace and stability across the Taiwan Strait.

4.4.2 The Contemporary Situation

The past five years have witnessed unprecedented levels of EU interest in, engagement with, and outspokenness regarding Taiwan. Importantly, there has been no change to the EU's official position on "One China," which the EEAS website today publicly defines as recognizing the PRC as "the sole legal government of China." Nevertheless, it emphasizes the EU and Taiwan's "solid relations and close cooperation," and "regular consultations." Regarding cross-Strait tensions, it stresses, "The EU has a strong stake in peace, security and stability in Asia"; "supports the status quo and peaceful resolution of differences across the Taiwan Strait, rejecting the use or threat of force"; and "continues to encourage dialogue and constructive engagement" (EEAS 2021a).

This coincides with Europe's souring view on China, especially since 2019, when the EU took the remarkable step of identifying China as not only a "partner" and "competitor," but also a "rival" (European Commission 2019). This followed the EP's first-ever debate on cross-Strait relations (European Parliament 2019), which eventually led to the first-ever official EP delegation to Taiwan, and the first-ever report on "EU-Taiwan relations." The latter, which was overwhelmingly approved in autumn 2021 (580 votes in favor; 26 against), called for "closer relations with Taiwan guided by the EU's One China policy"; named Taipei "a key EU partner and democratic ally"; "stressed the urgent need" for moves toward a bilateral investment agreement; expressed "grave concern" over China's "belligerence," "pressure," and "disinformation campaigns" against Taiwan; and called on the EU to "do more to address these tensions, to protect Taiwan's democracy, and the island's status as an important EU partner." It also proposed renaming the European Economic and Trade Office in Taipei to the "European Union Office in Taiwan" – "in order to reflect the broad scope of EU-Taiwanese ties" (European Parliament 2021). In July 2022, EP Vice President Nicole Beer led a historically high-level delegation to Taiwan, where they met with President Tsai and Foreign Minister Joseph Wu. In June 2023, Wu visited Poland, the Czech Republic, Italy, and Brussels, where he again met Beer. While in Prague, he even met the sitting Czech president (*Focus Taiwan* 2023; *Taipei Times* 2023).

The post-2019 period has also witnessed unprecedentedly frank and supportive rhetoric regarding Taiwan from the EC itself. In 2021, a speech written for High Representative for Foreign Affairs and Security Policy Josep Borrell (the EU's top foreign policy official) was titled "EU-Taiwan political relations and cooperation" – conspicuously exploding the myth that Taiwan's ties with Europe are strictly economic and commercial. Adopting language arguably even more assertive than the U.S. official position, which only calls for no *unilateral* changes to the status quo, it stated that Europeans "have an interest in preserving the status quo in the Taiwan Strait." It identified Taiwan as a "like-minded partner," observed that "exchanges and cooperation with Taiwan have intensified," and noted that the EU is Taiwan's largest foreign investor (Vestager 2021).

That same year, the EC's Indo-Pacific strategy mentioned Taiwan for the first time, identified it as a "partner" multiple times, and even linked the Taiwan Strait directly to "European security and prosperity" (European Commission 2021). In the wake of China's reaction to Pelosi's August 2022 visit, official rhetoric from President Ursula von der Leyen and Borrell have reinforced this idea. In various venues, including in joint statements with the United States and U.S. allies, and even during visits to Beijing, these leaders have repeatedly highlighted Europe's interest in maintaining the cross-Strait status quo.

For example, Borrell issued an unprecedented series of bold statements in April 2023. He stated that "any attempt to change the status quo by force would be unacceptable" (Borrell 2023a) and identified "Taiwan" as a "fundamental issue for Europe." Regarding the latter, he gave "three main reasons": the Taiwan Strait's significance for trade; "a takeover of Taiwan by force would of course be unacceptable in principle, but it would also be unacceptable in economic terms" given Taiwan's strategic role in the semiconductor industry; and Taiwan is part of the EU's "geostrategic perimeter" and if the EU wishes to be "a geopolitical power" it must "guarantee peace" and "defend our interests." Remarkably, he even called for European navies to conduct freedom of navigation operations (Borrell 2023b). Lastly, he argued in a French-language op-ed that the EU's position on "One China" is consistent but not unconditional, noting that related issues concern Europe "economically, commercially, and technologically." He even reiterated his call for "European navies to patrol the Taiwan Strait to signify Europe's commitment to freedom of navigation in this absolutely crucial area," and, in language that again seemed to go beyond the U.S. position, called for "enforcing" the status quo (Borrell 2023c).

Such remarkable statements from the EU's top foreign policy official suggest that – contrary to the EU's reputation as a primarily economic player – on issues related to Taiwan and maintenance of the cross-Strait status quo its leaders are increasingly eager to assert themselves, arguably even more so than leaders in most of its member states. That this has happened despite an institutional need for consensus, a vastly larger and more diverse array of member states today than in 1975, and the EU's conspicuously large economic interests in China makes this space an extremely important one to watch. The days when many European governments viewed Taiwan and the Taiwan Strait dismissively as "America's problem" or avoided putting related issues on the EU political and policy agenda appear to be gone.

Importantly, and despite Beijing's assertions to the contrary, EU leaders identify their rhetoric and policies as fully compatible with the EU's (intentionally vague) official position. What has changed in recent years is not the EU's position, per se, but rather the international and internal political environment that leads the consensus-based union to reinterpret what "One China" means for Europe *in practice*, especially as it concerns substantive policies and rhetoric vis-à-vis Taiwan and the Taiwan Strait.

That said, it is important not to exaggerate recent developments. As in other cases, politics and consideration of China's reactions still function as constraints on sensitive matters such as renaming the EU's office in Taipei or pursuing a bilateral investment treaty with Taiwan, which was reportedly put on ice after prospects for an EU-China trade deal emerged. Nevertheless, the long-term trend is clear: substantive and meaningful engagement with Taipei coupled with outspokenness on cross-Strait peace and stability are vastly greater today than in 1975, or even upon the EU's creation in 1993. That is true despite Brussels' officially unchanging position on "One China."

4.5 NATO

As a nongovernment treaty organization with "North Atlantic" in its official name, NATO understandably has no organizational position on "One China" or Taiwan. Furthermore, the treaty's famous Article 5 commitment – that an armed attack against any member obligates all members to assist the ally suffering the attack – legally applies only to "Europe or North America" (NATO 1949). Accordingly, one could argue that NATO should be excluded from the present study. As recently as a few years ago, that would have been entirely justifiable.

Developments since 2019, however, reveal growing strategic interest within NATO in Indo-Pacific affairs generally, and concerns about China's behavior specifically. The Taiwan Strait has also become a topic of both internal discussions and strikingly bold statements from NATO's secretary-general.

Regarding growing concerns within NATO about China, a historic turning point was reached in the London Declaration, which identified "China's growing influence and international policies" as "present[ing] both opportunities and challenges that we need to address together as an alliance" (NATO 2019). Since then, NATO has increased its attention on the Indo-Pacific, including by designating Australia, New Zealand, the ROK, and Japan as "Indo-Pacific partners" and inviting them to attend NATO summits and ministerial meetings. Such developments are particularly noteworthy because they require consensus among NATO's 30-plus members, many of whom have extensive economic, political, and other ties with China.

In 2022, Russia's full-scale invasion of Ukraine, which immediately followed Beijing and Moscow's announcement of a "no limits partnership," accelerated these trends. That June, NATO's Strategic Concept identified PRC "ambitions and coercive policies" as a "challenge" to member states' "interests, security and values" and stressed that the allies would "stand up for our shared values and the rules-based international order, including freedom of navigation" (NATO 2022). Although the new Strategic Concept did not mention Taiwan or the Taiwan Strait, China's large-scale military exercises around Taiwan two months later exacerbated concerns within NATO about the potential implications of a cross-Strait crisis for Euro-Atlantic security and the wider alliance. By year's end, the organization began discussing related issues for the first time (*Financial Times* 2022).

More conspicuously, in the wake of China's large-scale military exercises after Pelosi's visit to Taiwan, NATO's long-serving Secretary General Jens Stoltenberg (the former prime minister of Norway) became unprecedentedly outspoken on Taiwan-related issues. In a series of interviews in 2023, he stated that member states have "clearly communicated that the status quo in and around Taiwan should not be changed by force, and China's threatening rhetoric and behaviour against Taiwan is unjustified, and any differences and disputes around Taiwan should be solved by peaceful means" (NATO 2023). Linking security across regions, he argued that "Any attempt by China to try to change the status quo by the use of military force will have severe consequences for East Asia [and] for NATO allies and for global security" (*Nikkei Asia* 2023). And while stressing that NATO "will not become a global alliance with members from Asia," he has also noted that "any conflict in and around Taiwan will have profound consequences for all of us" (Editorial Board 2023).

Particularly striking was Stoltenberg's unusual 2023 joint statement with a leader from a non-NATO country, Japanese Prime Minister Kishida. It noted that "We strongly oppose any unilateral attempts to change the status quo by force or coercion in the East China Sea," "emphasize the importance of peace and stability across the Taiwan Strait as an indispensable element in security and prosperity in the international community," and "encourage a peaceful resolution of cross-Strait issues." Rather puzzlingly, it even included the following line: "*Our basic positions on Taiwan* remain unchanged" (Kishida and Stoltenberg 2023; emphasis added). (Although officials in Brussels confirm that NATO has no organizational position on Taiwan,[13] the fact that such a line was included with a foreign leader raises intriguing questions.)

Although none of this is to suggest NATO is considering a direct role in any potential cross-Strait conflict, it is clear that China and the Taiwan Strait are now – for the first time – legitimate topics of discussions within the organization. Given contemporary political realities, deepening concerns about Taiwan and the Taiwan Strait among U.S. European allies, and widespread expectations that the United States would respond if Beijing aggresses against Taiwan, this should not be surprising. The NATO Treaty's Article 4 states that "The Parties will consult together whenever, in the opinion of any of them, the territorial integrity, political independence or security of any of the Parties is threatened" (NATO 1949). It is not difficult to imagine a conflict triggering at least an

---

[13] Author's on-record email exchange with NATO official, August 2023.

Article 4 discussion and, potentially, a response from a coalition of willing NATO members. Even if NATO itself seems unlikely to get directly involved, it could support member states indirectly, such as by backfilling in Europe or the North Atlantic for U.S. and other members' military assets deployed to the Indo-Pacific.

In short, developments since 2019 make NATO's positioning and rhetoric vis-à-vis China and the Taiwan Strait an increasingly important space to watch.

4.6 Conclusion

This brief survey of the U.S. three most capable and wealthiest allies in Western Europe and the EU demonstrates that major European powers have long played important roles in supporting Taiwan's international space and cross-Strait peace and stability. Most significantly, upon recognizing Beijing, none of these governments endorsed Beijing's claim of sovereignty over Taiwan.

Nevertheless, the ambiguous official positions on "One China" each adopted then (or modified later) neither locked in nor were particularly predictive of each ally's subsequent approach vis-à-vis Taiwan and the Taiwan Strait thenceforth in any practical sense. On the contrary, the variability in approaches both across cases and within them evinces how each government has enjoyed significant flexibility to operationalize its effective Taiwan policy in accordance with political leaders' evolving assessments of the interests of the people it represents.

In making relevant policy judgments, leaders remained ever-mindful of the trade-offs and risks of backlash from China. That calculus can change in response to shifting political winds. Even France and Germany, whose respective 1994 and 2004 joint statements with Beijing appeared to reveal their leaders' willingness to make partial political concessions on language regarding "one China" in order to improve ties with Beijing, today appear eager to demonstrate that there is little daylight separating them from the United States and its other major democratic treaty allies. Indeed, the past few years have witnessed a remarkable trend toward relative convergence among the EU and major U.S. treaty allies and unprecedented degrees of discussion in their capitals regarding both Taiwan and the Taiwan Strait. Even NATO's secretary-general began adopting similar language.

Regardless, this section's empirical survey demonstrates a long-term and increasingly shared interest across much of Europe in bolstering "unofficial" ties with Taiwan, signaling solidarity with one another, and in contributing, at least rhetorically, to peace and stability across the Taiwan Strait. Though most of these efforts predated Pelosi's August 2022 visit to Taipei, the profound impact on European concerns of China's massive military exercises was captured in the EU High Representative's joint statement with G7 foreign ministers. It criticized China's actions as "aggressive," unjustified, and "destabilizing." Even so, the statement also emphasized that "there is no change in the respective one China policies, where applicable, and basic positions on Taiwan of the G7 members" (G7 2022).

These developments are not happening in a geopolitical or economic vacuum, however; nor is this all about Taiwan. The shift in perspectives across Europe appears to be heavily affected by concerns about China's "destabilizing" behavior more generally, increasingly mainstream recognition of the Indo-Pacific's importance for European interests, and, especially since 2022, the profound shift in concerns about major power conflict as a result of Russia's actions in Ukraine. As one illustrative example of the former, since the EU identified China as a "rival" in 2019, France, Germany, the UK, and the EU have all released strategic documents specific to the Indo-Pacific and/or China. Meanwhile, even NATO's consensus-based 2022 strategic concept identified PRC "ambitions and coercive policies" as a "challenge" to its members' "interests, security and values" (NATO 2022).

Though geography alone suggests that most European governments' potential roles in a cross-Strait military crisis would be limited primarily to diplomatic, economic, and political actions, manifold means exist for them to support Taiwan and the United States without the physical deployment of air, naval, or ground forces. European actors have a tremendous amount of both actual and potential influence, especially through their extensive trade and financial ties with China (e.g., possible sanctions). They might also take action in space/cyberspace and/or "backfill" for U.S. and other allied military assets in Europe or elsewhere in the world to make it easier for the United States (and possibly others) to concentrate forces in East Asia.

5 Discussion and Major Takeaways

Applied to the six wealthiest and most powerful U.S. democratic treaty allies in the Western Pacific and Europe, as well as the European Union and NATO, this Element's analytical framework facilitates a more nuanced understanding of allies' varied approaches to Taiwan, their contributions to Taiwan's international space and cross-Strait peace and stability, and the "One China" framework's complex operation in international politics, past and present. More generally, it also highlights the critically important, but oft-neglected or misunderstood, distinction between Beijing's self-defined "one-China principle" and key U.S. allies' intentionally ambiguous official positions regarding Taiwan's status. The headline takeaways are threefold:

First, U.S. allies have exercised far greater agency and played more significant roles in supporting Taiwan's international space and the post-1949 cross-Strait status quo than the overwhelmingly U.S.-centric academic and policy discourse generally suggests – in key instances even blazing trails Washington would later follow. None of this is to deny Washington's outsize significance as the primary external enabler of Taiwan's international space and cross-Strait peace and stability. But Taipei and Washington have not been alone. Had U.S. allies' leaders made different choices in the interest of scoring points with leaders in Beijing, the history of even U.S.-Taiwan relations after 1979 would almost certainly have played out differently. Put simply, the positions and policies of major U.S. democratic treaty allies have been an essential, albeit underappreciated, condition not only for peace and (relative) stability across the Taiwan Strait but also Taiwan's survival; its significant, if unofficial, ties with the world's wealthiest and most influential democratic powers; its robust and advanced economy; and its eventual emergence as the most liberal democratic polity in Asia.

Second, despite striking similarities in many U.S. allies' intentionally ambiguous official positions on Taiwan's status, how leaders choose to operationalize those positions has been highly variable, both across and within cases. Essential to understanding not only the U.S.' but also its key allies' positions and policies vis-à-vis Taiwan and the Taiwan Strait is the idea that the "One China" framework is an informal, flexible, institution. It is the ambiguity at its heart that today enables the deepening symbolically and practically significant engagement with Taiwan and proliferation of statements of opposition to "unilateral changes to the status quo," inter alia. Far from being locked in upon switching official recognition from the ROC to the PRC, in practice each allied government's effective Taiwan policy has been remarkably flexible. Short of official recognition of the ROC/Taiwan as a sovereign state, to a striking degree it is whatever its political leaders choose to make it. The extent to which a government develops pragmatic ties with or speaks out in support of Taiwan or cross-Strait peace and stability is a political choice, one which, of course, factors in, but is not necessarily beholden to, Beijing's preferences.

Third, as it concerns today: Beijing's increasingly coercive posture vis-à-vis Taipei, rapidly changing balances of power and influence across the Strait and wider region, growing international power and influence, and more brazen assertion of its "one-China principle" internationally all but guarantee that U.S. allies' policy choices will remain critical variables affecting the future of Taiwan's international space, peace and stability across the Taiwan Strait, the

U.S.' and Taiwan's own policy options in peacetime or a crisis, and democratic Taiwan's continued viability as a de facto autonomous actor. As this Element's case studies demonstrate, over the past several years many allies appear to be (re-)discovering their own agency and stakes in circumstances affecting democratic Taiwan. Most conspicuously, recent official statements from all major U.S. ally capitals leave no question that peace and stability across the Taiwan Strait is now generally considered a common challenge within East Asia *and beyond*.

A concise summary of several more general takeaways from this Element's empirical analysis follows:

5.1 No Major Democratic U.S. Ally Endorsed the PRC's Sovereignty Claim

Though generally acknowledged in the U.S.-China case, the myth of "consensus" at the "One China" framework's heart also manifests in the decades-old positions and policies of major U.S. allies. From London to Paris to Ottawa to Tokyo, political leaders' unwillingness to endorse Beijing's claim of sovereignty over Taiwan, coupled with the vagueness and flexibility at the heart of the "One China" idea, has enabled practically consequential variability and dynamism in major U.S. democratic treaty allies' respective positions on, and policies toward, Taiwan and the Taiwan Strait.

Simply put, and contrary to what Beijing and many others assert today, upon recognizing the PRC neither the United States nor any of its major democratic treaty allies endorsed Beijing's self-defined and asserted "one-China principle," an essential component of which is the idea that Taiwan is part of the PRC. After the 1964 France-PRC communique – which did not even mention Taiwan or "One China" – resulted in Paris briefly having diplomatic relations with both "Chinas," Beijing insisted that governments that wished to normalize diplomatic relations must recognize the PRC as the "sole legal government of China."[14] Nevertheless, beginning with Canada in 1970 all major democratic U.S. treaty allies carefully avoided taking an unambiguous position on the sovereignty question in their bilateral communiques with Beijing. Typically, they merely noted "understanding," "respect," or "acknowledgment" that *Beijing claimed* sovereignty, without endorsing that claim.

When considering the implications of those intentionally ambiguous positions for the contemporary status quo, it is also important to recall that many

---

[14] As noted in Section 4, the exception among U.S. allies after 1970 was the FRG in 1972. For reasons unique to its own Cold War–era division, Bonn negotiated a communique that mentioned neither Taiwan nor East Germany.

allied governments considered the question of whether to recognize the then-authoritarian ROC regime in Taiwan distinct from the question of whether *Taiwan* and the people there "belonged" to either "China." Not only had numerous allies actively sought a "two Chinas" or "one China, one Taiwan" solution before 1972, governments such as the United States and UK had long considered Taiwan's status an "undetermined" international issue. In several cases, declassified internal documents confirm that several allied governments rejected Beijing's pressure to recognize its sovereignty claim based on the hope that future circumstances might allow self-determination for the people on Taiwan and official recognition of their government in some form. In short, political leaders' pragmatic decisions to switch recognition of "the government of China" from the (then-) authoritarian and deeply unpopular ROC regime in Taipei to the authoritarian communist government on the mainland was not tantamount to endorsing the PRC's claim of sovereignty over Taiwan. Widespread assertions to the contrary are ahistorical and based on a logical fallacy. This oft-overlooked distinction is fundamental to the ambiguity of the U.S. and various allies' positions on "One China."

In understanding the origins of allies' positions on "One China," it is also important to recall that all but one of the cases examined in this Element recognized the PRC regime during the 1950s, 1960s, or 1970s – a period when authoritarian single-party governments in both Beijing and Taipei categorically rejected potential alternative solutions to the cross-Strait dispute, including "Two Chinas," or "one China, one Taiwan." Thus, it was not just Beijing but also Taipei that forced all U.S. allies to choose "one [and only one] 'China.'" As Bush notes, the world will never know whether, if the KMT had been more receptive to U.S. and others' efforts to facilitate dual presence in the UN for both the PRC and ROC earlier, Taiwan might today enjoy far greater international recognition, including more representation in international organizations (Bush 2004, 120).

5.2 U.S. Allies' Agency, Trailblazing, and Significance Historically and Today

When it comes to Taiwan's international space and cross-Strait peace and stability, allies have exercised underappreciated but important leadership in at least two major ways. First, consider the counterfactual: if the many allies that recognized Beijing long before the United States did had given in to PRC pressure to endorse its claim of sovereignty over Taiwan, it seems quite plausible that Washington's own options would have been severely limited by the time its leaders initiated normalization negotiations with Beijing in the

1970s. Second, although the United States has always been the ROC/Taiwan's most important external partner, even after recognizing the PRC several U.S. allies played foundational roles in defining, incrementally stretching, and consolidating the effective bounds of what could in practice constitute politically acceptable "unofficial" or "nongovernmental" engagement with Taiwan. In key instances, creative precedents set by allies even provided the models from which the United States would later borrow. In aggregate, these actions have proven essential for Taiwan's successful efforts to survive as an autonomous international political actor (albeit with significant constraints); develop robust, comprehensive, and practically significant (if nominally unofficial) links to the wealthiest and most powerful democratic countries in the Western Pacific and Europe, and eventually emerge as both an economic powerhouse and the first and only democracy in the primarily Chinese-speaking world.

Of particular significance were the trail-blazing actions of four U.S. allies: the UK, France, Canada, and Japan.

In January 1950, the UK set foundational precedents not only for a major Western power to establish diplomatic relations with the nascent PRC government, but also to do so without recognizing Beijing's claim to Taiwan. Significantly, London did so while maintaining meaningful cooperation with the ROC government, and while exploring various measures to keep Taiwan out of Communist control. The UK's letter unilaterally announced recognition without mentioning "Taiwan," and London refused to shut down its consulate in Tamsui, inter alia. This was a concrete realization of a view shared by many foreign governments at the time: on the one hand, recognizing that the Communists had effectively won the Chinese civil war and controlled "the mainland," but treating the question of whether Taiwan was part of the newly established PRC as a separate issue. Internally, London reconciled these views by settling on a position that considered Taiwan's status "undetermined" and kept all options for Taiwan's future on the table, including the continuation of KMT rule, independent statehood, or a UN trusteeship (Tsang 1994, 105, 108).

France in 1964 became the first Western government to sign a bilateral communique and exchange ambassadors with Beijing. But it did so without severing ties with Taipei or committing to the PRC's version of the "one-China principle." The 1964 France-PRC communique did not even mention "Taiwan," much less endorse Beijing's claim of sovereignty over it. It was ultimately the ROC government, not France, that severed diplomatic ties in accordance with its own "one-China principle"; accordingly, France had diplomatic ties with *both* Chinas for a few weeks. This was a concrete demonstration that the only reason a "two Chinas" or "one China, one Taiwan" resolution of the cross-Strait dispute was impossible was *politics*; that is, at the time, Beijing's and Taipei's refusal to accept mutual recognition in any form. France would again become a trailblazer a quarter century later, when the Cold War's end, Beijing's brutal globally-televised 1989 crackdown on unarmed protesters, and Taiwan's democratization, inter alia, led various governments to expand the nature and extent of their officially "unofficial" engagement with Taipei. During the 1991–1993 period, for example, Paris even allowed French firms to sell Taiwan naval frigates and fighter jets and began sending to Taipei government officials higher in rank than any Washington would allow at the time.

In 1970 Canadian negotiators invented a new formula that creatively met the PRC's post-1964 condition – that normalization communiques refer explicitly to "Taiwan" and "One China" – while avoiding endorsement of the PRC's sovereignty claim. In October 1970 – nine months *before* Henry Kissinger's secret July 1971 visit to China and Nixon's subsequent public announcement of his plans to visit – Canada became the first government of a U.S. ally to normalize relations with Beijing through a bilateral communique in which it mentioned but – critically – agreed only to "take note of" the PRC's claim to Taiwan. This strikingly ambiguous "Canadian formula" – which neither endorsed nor challenged Beijing's "one-China principle" – was immediately adopted by Italy and Belgium. It also became the basic template for the U.S. and other democratic treaty allies' subsequent normalization communiques with Beijing.

In the September 1972 Japan–PRC normalization communique, Tokyo also refused to take a legal position on Taiwan's status. But it was Japan's subsequent *operationalization* of its non-position that blazed multiple trails for others – including the United States – to follow. First, even after recognizing Beijing Tokyo insisted on maintaining a euphemistically named "Exchange Association" in Taipei to enable practical engagement through nominally nongovernmental actors. Second, Japan's ruling Liberal Democratic Party partnered with the ruling KMT in Taiwan to create a robust "political" pipeline for regular exchanges between legislators as an alternative to direct government–government official contacts. Third, Tokyo established a public position that "issues relating to Taiwan be resolved peacefully" through cross-Strait dialogue.

These three 1970s innovations became models for the United States and many others, with long-term consequences. Exchanges of legislators and calls for "peaceful resolution" of the cross-Strait dispute are now commonplace among major U.S. allies. Meanwhile, Japan's "Exchange Association" set the precedent not only for the U.S. much more famous AIT in 1979, but also the de facto representative offices in Taipei established by other U.S. allies. As demonstrated in Sections 3 and 4, most of these offices have gradually taken on many roles of official embassies elsewhere, and have become staffed by increasingly senior government officials and professional diplomats. Although the degree of official candor about this reality today varies, three examples are revealing: Since 1993, the official name of Seoul's office is the "Korean Mission in Taipei" – "mission" being a term with clear diplomatic connotations. Whereas Canada's foreign ministry officially calls its office a "Trade Office" its own website notes that it is "now deliver[ing] the same services as Canada's *other missions* abroad" ("Canadian Trade Office in Taipei, Taiwan" 2022). For its part, the EU's diplomatic service describes its "Economic and Trade Office" in Taipei as "the official representation of the Europe Union in Taiwan" (EEAS 2021b).[15] Regardless of the public "form" each government presents to the world, the de facto, if not literal, "officiality" of most such offices, as well as the degree, nature, and extent of their substantive engagement with Taiwan they facilitate, has quietly expanded over time – belying the convenient fiction that each government's bilateral engagement with Taiwan is merely "economic and cultural."

5.3 Practically Flexible Ambiguity: "Officiality" Is in the Eye of the Beholder

As the aforementioned examples illustrate, in the absence of official diplomatic relations, defining what each government's "unofficial," or "nongovernmental," relations with Taiwan look like in practice, as well as where the effective bounds on "appropriate" engagement, rhetoric, and/or policy should lie, is left up to political leaders to decide. Similar to the U.S. case highlighted by Bush (2017, 15–18) four factors generally affect how far allied political leaders decide to push the envelope: consideration of national interests, expected reaction from Beijing, Taiwan's own policies, and domestic political pressures.

As Sections 3 and 4 attest, the historical evolution of key allies' effective Taiwan policies is neither inherently unidirectional nor uniform across cases. Today, however, many political leaders appear more willing to deepen practical engagement with Taipei and publicly express support for its international space and cross-Strait peace and stability. Recent years have witnessed new developments that even two decades ago – under very different political circumstances – leaders would have dismissed as too suggestive of "officiality" and therefore beyond the bounds of appropriateness. All this despite officially unchanging, decades-old positions on "One China."

The empirical record suggests that where Beijing draws the line on "officiality" – and what it will grudgingly tolerate in practice, regardless of what it says publicly – also varies. Four brief examples help illustrate these points. (1) Since the 1980s, and many years after switching official diplomatic recognition from Taipei to Beijing, multiple U.S. allies have

---

[15] Emphasis added in both cases.

newly established and gradually upgraded their de facto representation in Taiwan, and/or authorized increasingly high-level exchanges with officials from Taiwan – including sitting Cabinet ministers. As one largely symbolic example, many diplomats posted in Taipei now even use foreign ministry email addresses. (2) Power dynamics are also at play. For instance, whereas in 2021 Beijing subjected tiny Lithuania to a downgrade of diplomatic relations and severe economic sanctions after its government allowed Taipei to use the word "Taiwan" in the official name of its "Taiwan Representative Office" in Vilnius, there was no major fallout when Japan in 2017 quietly added "Japan-Taiwan" to the formal name of its "Exchange Association" in Taipei. (3) Third, only one generation ago visas for people from Taiwan were so controversial that the UK issued them on a separate sheet of paper (Reilly 2020, 99). (4) Recent years have also witnessed a surge of legislative exchanges, which Beijing often decries as "official" and alleged "violations" of allies' "One China" policies. Most allies clearly disagree. For example, despite repeated assertions from the PRC's embassy in Berlin that Germany "is not allowed to have any official contacts with Taiwan, and that also applies to German parliamentarians," in 2023 multiple parliamentary delegations and, for the first time in a quarter-century, a German cabinet minister visited Taipei. These are but a few examples of the objectively measurable shifting and politically defined bounds of "unofficial," or "nongovernmental," engagement with Taiwan.

5.4 The Politically Contingent Variability of Allies' Effective Taiwan Policies

How key U.S. allies have chosen to operationalize their effective policy toward Taiwan and the Taiwan Strait has been (1) diverse across cases and (2) variable over time. Indeed, regardless of the similarities in allies' ambiguous official decades-old positions on "One China," Sections 3 and 4 reveal striking variability in how and when political leaders have chosen to operationalize that position in terms of rhetoric, policies, and the extent and nature of engagement with Taiwan. This observation, in turn, highlights the necessity of this study's two-step analytical framework. After all, if key U.S. allies' positions on "One China" are similar and static across decades, but their practical policies vis-à-vis Taiwan and the Taiwan Strait vary across cases and over time, then, logically, the former cannot fully explain the latter. Rather, something else must be at work.

That it is domestic and international political vicissitudes and leaders' judgments, not (nonexistent) legally binding or explicit commitments to Beijing, that largely shape the dynamic contours of U.S. allies' policies vis-à-vis Taiwan helps clarify why in practice they can vary so widely. One real-world implication: the frequently heard refrain that "Country X 'cannot' do Y because of its 'One China' policy or position on 'One China'" should typically not be accepted at face value. In many cases, it is best understood as masking a political judgment about whether a given action or statement is advisable. As noted earlier, what may be a bridge too far for one government or political leader, or in one historical context, may be feasible or even desirable for, or in, another. In short, how leaders choose to interpret "officiality" and where the "line" is have always been heavily politically contingent. A few brief examples from Sections 3 and 4, respectively, help illustrate variability across and within cases.

5.4.1 Variation across Cases

Whereas Step 1 of this study's analytical framework reveals that Japan, Australia, and the ROK have similarly ambiguous official positions on "One China," Step 2 demonstrates that their approaches toward Taiwan- and cross-Strait-related issues vary in practically significant ways. Though there is greater convergence among allies in recent years than decades ago (itself a testament to the theme of Section 5.4.2), important differences persist in the extent and nature of bilateral engagement and outspokenness in support of Taiwan's international space and cross-Strait peace and stability. For instance, Tokyo in recent years demonstrates a willingness to take some steps – for example, expressing clear support for Taiwan to join CPTPP and dispatching a de facto defense attaché to its office in Taipei – that Canberra has not. On the other hand, until recently Canberra had a history of sending Cabinet ministers to Taipei. And it has for years quietly conducted naval transits of the Taiwan Strait – the latter something Japan had not done until just before this Element went to press.

Meanwhile, despite Seoul being the only U.S. treaty ally bold enough to call both its representative office in Taipei and Taipei's office in Seoul "missions" – something even Washington did not do after switching recognition – Korean political leaders typically stand out for their relatively greater reluctance to take overtly public stands in support of Taiwan, its international space, or deepening bilateral ties. In addition to the examples noted in Section 3, Korea is also the only allied government examined in this Element not to have conducted a Taiwan Strait transit. Although since 2021 Seoul has become newly vocal about "the importance of peace and stability in the Taiwan Strait," its public rhetoric in this regard remains relatively anodyne. Government officials generally avoid potentially controversial expressions of support of Taipei or criticism of Beijing.

These brief examples illustrate not only variation across cases but also the importance of analytically differentiating between an ally's abstract official position on "One China" and its rhetoric and practical policies vis-à-vis Taiwan and the Taiwan Strait. In all three Western Pacific cases, the crucial factor is not a static decades-old position on Taiwan's status but successive democratically elected political leaders' judgments about what best serves their country's interests. Given Seoul's unique geopolitical situation, an understandable desire not to risk overly antagonizing Beijing – its huge and powerful next-door neighbor, most important trading partner, and essential partner for addressing Seoul's manifold concerns regarding North Korea – appears to loom particularly large in Korean leaders' political calculus and helps explain its relatively greater caution on Taiwan-related matters.

5.4.2 Variation within Cases (i.e., over Time)

Particular countries' effective policies toward Taiwan and the Taiwan Strait also vary meaningfully over time. Put simply, shifting domestic and international political winds can cause political leaders in one country to intermittently reevaluate the pros and cons of more robust engagement with Taipei, and to consider changing effective approaches accordingly.

The case of France exemplifies practically significant variation within a single case.

As discussed in Section 4, Paris' 1964 recognition of the PRC did not prevent French leaders from (eventually) significantly deepening ties with Taiwan. These efforts accelerated after 1989 against the backdrop of the Cold War's end, Taiwan's rapid democratization and economic development, and Beijing's June crackdown on protestors. During the 1989–1993 period, France allowed the sitting ROC foreign minister to visit Paris; renamed and upgraded its de facto representative office in Taipei; became the first foreign government recognizing the PRC to send a cabinet minister to Taiwan (something not even Washington had done); and approved sales to Taiwan of fighter jets and frigates (a historical fact that undermines the widespread misconception today that only the United States has sold major military platforms to Taiwan). Yet shifting domestic and international political winds soon catalyzed a symbolic course correction. After the arms sales fomented major political and economic backlash from the PRC, and with a new government in France ogling China's rapidly growing potential as an export market, in January 1994 Paris made a major concession to Beijing: it negotiated a new bilateral communique that took the remarkable steps of explicitly recognizing Taiwan as part of "Chinese territory" and pledging "not to authorize French companies to participate in the armament of Taiwan" (Ministère des Affaires étrangères 1994). Yet even the "new" 1994 position on "One China" did not cause Paris to undo or reverse the past deepening of "unofficial" France-Taiwan relations. Nor has that now three-decade-old political document prevented the Macron government from making the French government the first in Europe to mention Taiwan in a new Indo-Pacific strategy, to order the French navy to conduct multiple Taiwan Strait transits, to issue multiple official statements supporting Taiwan's "meaningful participation" in international organizations, and to call for "deepening relations with Taiwan." Nor did it stop Macron's policy advisor in 2023 from asserting that "the key components" of France's "Taiwan policy ... are exactly the same as the U.S.," and even threatening "massive sanctions" if China took action against Taiwan.

In sum, regardless of abstract official positions on "One China," how the United States and other key U.S. allies/partners choose to define, interpret, and operationalize their respective positions and policies vis-à-vis Taiwan are based on political judgments, themselves subject to changing domestic and international political forces and shifting evaluations of national interest. Thus, even those allies with strikingly similar official positions on Taiwan's status manifest approaches to Taiwan that are (1) diverse across cases; and (2) variable (within each case) over time.

5.5 Worsening Dis/Misinformation Exacerbates an Already Confused Public Discourse

Recent years have witnessed increasingly assertive and misleading propaganda from Beijing that appears designed to exploit both intentional ambiguity in the U.S. and its allies' actual positions on "One China" and widespread ignorance about them in order to shape overseas public and policy discourse regarding Taiwan to align with Beijing's preferred narrative and interests. Of particular consequence are efforts to unilaterally and retroactively define for the United States and its key allies what their respective "One China" policies are, as well as what rhetoric or activities constitute alleged "violations" thereof.

Such disinformation has found strikingly fertile ground in which to take root. Reasons are manifold, but three appear particularly salient today: First, the U.S. and key ally governments have traditionally seen differences with Beijing regarding "One China" as potentially incendiary political conflicts to be avoided in the interest of relations with the PRC and cross-Strait stability. Because – to borrow from Romberg's (2003, 48) observation regarding the United States – most allies' preference has long been to quietly do more than they say, whereas Beijing's approach is typically the opposite, the net effect is to cede much of the public discourse to China. This modus operandi exacerbates a second issue: Regardless of intent, ahistorical and misleading media, political, and even some scholarly commentaries often muddle or overlook the nuanced ambiguity baked into the U.S. and its major allies' official positions. Third, generational change and years of underinvestment in cross-Strait and Taiwan expertise across governments and academia – even among those focused on China and East Asia – further exacerbate the problem.

The net result is widespread misunderstanding, sometimes even among political leaders and policymakers themselves. Imprecision, misspeaking, and a lack of messaging discipline manifest both publicly and behind closed doors. Recent examples of the former abound. Australia's then-Prime Minister Scott Morrison apparently mixed up Australia's "One China policy" with Beijing's "One Country, Two Systems" – the latter the PRC's preferred nomenclature for its governance of Hong Kong, and aspirationally for Taiwan – when answering an interview question about Taiwan (*The Guardian* 2021). That same year, Japan's Prime Minister Suga Yoshihide referred to Taiwan as a "country" during parliamentary debate (TBS 2021). For its part, the European Commission referred to Taiwan as a "country" multiple times in its 1994 Asia Strategy (European Commission 1994). And in a striking public admission of confusion about the UK's own Taiwan policy even within the government, a 2023 Parliament report called for it "to be better understood across Whitehall departments to prevent policymakers from misspeaking or acting over-cautiously" (House of Commons (UK) 2023).

The point here is not to take a position on those statements, but to highlight the remarkably high noise:signal ratio in much contemporary public discourse, which often confuses more than it enlightens.

6 Conclusion

In a 2019 article on U.S.-China relations soberly titled "Competition without Catastrophe," Kurt Campbell and Jake Sullivan – leading architects of the Biden Administration's Indo-Pacific strategy – wrote, "Taiwan is not only a potential flash point; it is also the greatest unclaimed success in the history of U.S.-Chinese relations. The island has grown, prospered, and democratized in the ambiguous space between the United States and China as a result of the flexible and nuanced approach generally adopted by both sides" (Campbell and Sullivan 2019, 101–2). Although their intended point is sound, and the United States has been Taiwan's most important partner and de facto security benefactor throughout the post-1949 period, this passage also exemplifies the excessively U.S.-centric framing that has for decades permeated academic and policy discussions on the enabling factors behind Taiwan's international space and peace and stability across the Taiwan Strait.

This has not only been an issue among American policymakers and scholars, nor is it limited to the many analyses that have ignored allies entirely. As two cases in point: only two decades ago some leading non-U.S. experts suggested in studies specifically focused on other governments' engagement with Taiwan that major U.S. allies in Asia and Europe were disinterested and inflexible about engaging Taiwan due to their official positions on "One China." For example, a 2001 study by a Japanese expert contended that Tokyo's "1972 system" was so inflexible that it required Japan to "abstain[] from *any actions that Beijing opposes*, even though they may not violate the communique" (Amae 2001, emphasis added). The following year, an otherwise enlightening analysis by one of Europe's most prominent experts on Taiwan opened with an assertion that "all European countries['] . . . non-official ties with Taiwan . . . are limited to the economic and cultural sphere and should leave aside any move or transaction suggesting that Taiwan is anything else than a part of China under the PRC's rule." It further claimed that "the question of peaceful resolution of the Sino-Taiwanese dispute has never triggered any debate in Europe," that "democratization in Taiwan is unlikely to enhance Taipei's leverage in international relations," and that since ROC representatives lost their UN seat in 1971, "only the United States has expressed concern for the future of Taiwan" (Mengin 2002, 136).

Yet such narratives often downplay or overlook the agency and significance of major U.S. democratic treaty allies in facilitating both Taiwan's international space and peace and stability across the Taiwan Strait – before and after recognizing the PRC. By the time the U.S. government normalized diplomatic relations with China in 1979, every other major democratic U.S. treaty ally already had an ambassador in Beijing.[16] Even so, London, Paris, Ottawa, Tokyo, and other U.S. allied governments switched recognition from the ROC to the PRC without endorsing Beijing's claim of sovereignty over Taiwan. Of particular significance: In several cases, part of the original logic was to keep options open for an alternative resolution to the cross-Strait dispute if future circumstances were ever to allow it. And in the decades since, key allies have pushed the boundaries of "unofficial" engagement with Taiwan – in ways that both the United States and its other allies would later follow.

The cases examined within this Element are by no means exhaustive of the diverse histories and approaches vis-à-vis "One China," Taiwan, and the Taiwan Strait among the U.S.' more than three-dozen treaty allies in Europe and the Indo-Pacific, much less major non-ally partners like Singapore and India. Nonetheless, as highlighted in Section 5, they are sufficient for drawing several major takeaways beyond the most obvious fact that, Beijing's and others' widespread claims to the contrary, neither during the Cold War nor

---

[16] As noted elsewhere, South Korea was not a full democracy until the 1980s.

today has there ever been a "universal consensus" regarding what "One China" means or what Taiwan's relationship to "China" (or the PRC, specifically) is or should be.

Beijing's increasingly coercive approach toward Taiwan and its international partners since the DPP recaptured Taiwan's presidency in 2016 – coupled with President Tsai Ing-wen's (2016–2024) commitment to maintaining the cross-Strait status quo during her eight years in office – has catalyzed yet another shift among the U.S. and its allies toward more concern about Taiwan, its international space, and cross-Strait peace and stability, arguably than ever before. The result is a paradox: although since 2016 the number of foreign governments officially recognizing the ROC has reached an all-time low – from twenty-one then to twelve as of late 2024 – the practically consequential, if officially "unofficial," ties between Taiwan and the United States and its major democratic treaty allies have never been greater. In short, Beijing's ever-more assertive campaign to claim and "enforce" an alleged universal consensus that does not exist may be consolidating an emerging consensus among key U.S. democratic treaty allies (and the EU), actively encouraged by both Taipei and Washington, that they must be more vocal about their official positions on Taiwan and push back against Beijing's disinformation. In so doing, they effectively undermine parts of China's preferred narrative that assert that only Washington cares about Taiwan, and that U.S. support is merely a "card" the true intention of which is to "contain" China's rise.

The current historical moment is in many ways unique. Never before has China enjoyed such a favorable balance of power across the Taiwan Strait, making the threat of large-scale military action against Taiwan very real. Never before have China and Taiwan been so enmeshed in the global economy and supply chains on which the world depends. And never before has Taiwan been the most liberal democracy in Asia. Nevertheless, this is also not the first time that there has been an observable swing in major U.S. allies' interest in and engagement with Taiwan.

The sheer number of cases as well as the diversity of their historical, political, economic, and geographical circumstances caution against any simplistic one-size-fits-all generalizations about causality across time or space. After all, governments as varied as Tokyo, Seoul, and Berlin have different strategic priorities and post-1949 histories with both China and Taiwan/the ROC. Nevertheless, and especially in the post–Cold War period, the cases examined in this Element generally suggest a recurring, if complex, interplay of ideological, economic, and geopolitical considerations as key drivers. Especially of late, as China's rapidly growing military power makes the threat of a blockade or invasion unprecedentedly credible, allies' behavior vis-à-vis Taiwan and the

Taiwan Strait is also increasingly shaped by judgments about what rhetoric and policies can both protect Taiwan's de facto autonomy while also deterring a unilateral change to the status quo.

For instance, ideological, economic, and geopolitical factors manifest across several cases as drivers of remarkable late 1980s/early 1990s swings toward greater engagement with Taiwan. Against the backdrop of transformative change heralded by the end of the Cold War, multiple leaders contrasted Taipei's rapid democratization with Beijing's violent crackdown on unarmed civilians in June 1989, at the same time as decades of rapid industrialization and economic growth had transformed Taiwan into an increasingly attractive economic partner. Later in the 1990s and into the early aughts, by contrast, China appeared to be liberalizing, the narrative of "China's peaceful rise" was ascendant internationally, and leaders around the world coveted China's rapidly growing economy and massive population of 1.4 billion consumers (~60 times the size of Taiwan's). Meanwhile, many leaders distanced themselves from Taipei during the presidency of Chen Shui-bian (2000–2008), who was widely seen as flirting with a de jure declaration of independence that risked provoking a conflict. After Chen left office in 2008 the continuing appeal of closer economic and other ties with China, coupled with remarkable expansion of cross-Strait cooperation and stability during the presidency of Ma Ying-jeou (2008–2016), sharply reduced concerns about a possible crisis.

In stark contrast to that earlier period, the past several years have been marked by a surge in negative views of Beijing in every major U.S. ally (e.g., Pew 2023), worsening bilateral relations with China nearly across-the-board, and a general sense that it is Xi Jinping's increasingly authoritarian CCP-led government, not the relatively moderate post-2016 DPP administrations in democratic Taipei, that is attempting to unilaterally change the status quo. Especially salient since 2022 – the year of Russia's full-scale invasion of Ukraine and unprecedentedly massive PLA military exercises around Taiwan in the wake of Pelosi's peaceful visit – is a widespread sense that the risk of a catastrophic war or other calamity of global consequence is real; accordingly, leaders must be more proactive in signaling their support for the cross-Strait status quo.

As explored in greater detail in Section 4, recent developments in the far-off European Union offer compelling examples of how sharply perspectives on China (and Taiwan) have shifted among major democratic U.S. allies and partners – clearly marking the current moment as a new era.

Of particular note, in May 2023, Ursula von der Leyen, president of the European Commission – hardly an institution with a reputation as an outspoken geopolitical actor – suggested the major shift in European perspectives and policies is due to Beijing's own actions, stating, "Our [EU] policies toward China need to change because China has changed." She continued, "we reaffirm our unwavering commitment to peace and stability in the Taiwan Strait. We are collectively opposing any unilateral change to the status quo, particularly by force" (von der Leyen 2023). This statement from von der Leyen followed a remarkably assertive op-ed by the Commission's Vice President, Josep Borrell. Not only did it have the revealing title "A Cold Look at China" (*Un Regard Froid Sur La Chine*), but the short piece also devoted a full paragraph to Taiwan. It even took the remarkable step of "calling on European navies to patrol the Taiwan Strait to signify Europe's commitment to freedom of navigation in this absolutely crucial area" (Borrell 2023c).

Consistent with this Element's recurring analytical theme, EU leaders today consider such rhetoric, repeated legislative exchanges, and other recent efforts to deepen support for Taiwan and cross-Strait peace and stability fully compatible with the EU's 1975 position on "One China." What has changed in recent years is not that position (the form), but rather the international and internal political environment that now leads the 27-member consensus-based bloc to reinterpret how that vague position should be operationalized in substantive rhetoric and policy vis-à-vis Taiwan and the Taiwan Strait. The overriding objective is roughly consistent with that of the United States and most other U.S. allies: deterring unilateral changes to the status quo, supporting democratic Taiwan's international space, and encouraging a peaceful resolution of the cross-Strait dispute.

6.1 Toward an Uncertain Future

Two years after the PLA's unprecedentedly large-scale August 2022 exercises, such military and other forms of PRC pressure on Taiwan are now a conspicuously new normal. Beijing appears determined to use its growing power and influence to increasingly "squeeze" Taiwan and assert its self-defined "one-China principle," both across the Strait and internationally.

Where this all leads remains to be seen. Although recent years reveal an unmistakable trend among the U.S. and its major democratic treaty allies toward increasing concern about democratic Taiwan and cross-Strait peace and stability, this study also shows that the history of U.S. allied interest in and engagement with Taiwan is not always linear or unidirectional. Beijing has far more leverage internationally – both carrots and sticks – today than it did in the past. And it has not been shy about using it in pursuit of what its leaders consider "the core of China's core interests." In addition to pressure on the United States and its allies, in recent years many other foreign governments (e.g., across "the

Global South") appear willing to accommodate the PRC's preferences on Taiwan, such as agreeing to new joint statements endorsing Beijing's "one-China principle" and/or "unification." Of particular note is Russia, whose deepening military cooperation with China the U.S. intelligence community has publicly assessed may have implications for a cross-Strait conflict (Bloomberg 2024b).

Though this study's core research question required a narrow analytical focus on a few major U.S. democratic treaty allies, when thinking of future possibilities in the real world the greatest agency of course lies with Beijing and Taipei. For example, were Beijing tomorrow to abandon its sovereignty claim, or even forswore threats of force or coercion, the risks of a cross-Strait conflict would effectively disappear. Conversely, Taipei's possible future acquiescence to unification – in some form – would also fundamentally transform dynamics. So, too, potentially, could a leadership in Taiwan that brazenly pursues moves toward a de jure declaration of independence.

At present, of course, these scenarios seem unlikely. Regarding the latter, for years public opinion polls have consistently shown that the overwhelming majority of people in democratic Taiwan support the status quo (Election Study Center 2024). Meanwhile, against the backdrop of worsening ties between China and the United States and most of its allies, which Xi Jinping accuses of "all-around containment, encirclement and suppression of China" (*Renmin Ribao* 2023), it is difficult to be optimistic about Beijing changing its approach. On Taiwan, Beijing's position is clear: As articulated by China's foreign minister at the 2022 UN General Assembly, "Only when China is fully reunified can there be true peace across the Taiwan Strait," and it will "take the most forceful steps to oppose external interference" (*Associated Press* 2022). For good measure, a unilateral PRC readout of a June 2023 meeting with Secretary Blinken demanded that Washington "abide by the one-China principle," adding that "On the Taiwan question, China has no room for compromise or concession" (MFA (PRC) 2023). Beijing's increasingly proactive, even brazen, efforts to redefine for the United States and allies what their "One China" positions are, to rewrite the original meaning of UN 2758, to continue a freezeout of Taiwan's two most recent (DPP) presidents, and to peel off Taiwan's few remaining diplomatic allies, not to mention the CIA-confirmed order by Xi calling on the PLA to "be ready" by 2027 and major escalation in direct coercive military and other forms of pressure on Taiwan, make for a potentially incendiary cocktail.

Though based on some metrics the current historical moment marks a post-normalization high point in U.S. and allied support for Taiwan, the fundamentally political nature of the dynamics at play means it is hardly inevitable that current trends will continue. Especially with 2024 seeing major elections not only in Taiwan and the United States but also Japan, the UK, the EU, and many other capitals, both cross-Strait dynamics and the U.S. and its major allies' positions and policies vis-à-vis Taiwan will remain extremely important spaces to watch in the years ahead. Accordingly, scholars should update this Element's analysis in response to real-world developments. They should also consider applying this study's analytical framework to additional allied cases, especially the remaining G7 members (Canada and Italy), the Philippines, and other notable cases in Europe (e.g., small Eastern European countries such as Lithuania and the Czech Republic that are now among the most outspoken in support of Taiwan). Applying it to other major U.S. non-ally partners, especially India, may also be enlightening.

As this Element goes to press, multiple factors conspire to present the "One China" framework, to say nothing of Taiwan and its international partners, with arguably its greatest challenge since the 1970s. Needless to say, under the second Trump administration the extent of America's proactive engagement and leadership, support for Taiwan, and efforts to bolster deterrence and facilitate solidarity among U.S. allies and partners will all be critical variables. The outgoing Biden administration's Indo-Pacific strategy – under the leadership of Sullivan and Campbell, it should be noted – has been remarkably successful in these regards. It remains to be seen what approach the next president will take not only toward Taiwan and the Taiwan Strait, but also toward allies more generally. Though much is uncertain, one reality will not change: U.S. allies will – for better or worse – still have extremely consequential roles to play in shaping the future.

With both cross-Strait frictions and Beijing's relations with the United States, the EU, and many major U.S. democratic allies in a period of peak tension, and against the backdrop of major shifts in the balance of power and influence, both democratic Taiwan and cross-Strait peace and stability face unprecedentedly complicated challenges. Whether the United States and Taipei's other international partners can help sustain the status quo in the short term and, potentially, facilitate a peaceful, uncoerced, and mutually acceptable resolution of the cross-Strait dispute that allows the twenty-three million people who live in Taiwan to decide their future course much further down the line remain open questions. One thing is certain, however: The extremely important roles that major democratic U.S. treaty allies (and the EU) will have to play in shaping the future should be a consistent focus of both scholars or policymakers. The stakes for the people in democratic Taiwan, regional peace and stability, China's foreign relations, the international order, and the global economy could hardly be greater.

References

AFP. 2021. "UK Sends Warship Through Taiwan Strait for First Time in More than a Decade." September 27. www.theguardian.com/uk-news/2021/sep/28/uk-sends-warship-through-taiwan-straight-for-first-time-in-more-than-a-decade.

AIT. 1979. "U.S.-PRC Joint Communique." American Institute in Taiwan. January 1. www.ait.org.tw/our-relationship/policy-history/key-u-s-foreign-policy-documents-region/u-s-prc-joint-communique-1979/.

Amae, Yoshihisa. 2001. "Japan's Taiwan Policy: Beyond the 1972 System?" In *Taiwan's Presidential Politics*, edited by Muthiah Alagappa, 260–82. New York: Routledge.

American Institute in Taiwan. 2022. "Integrated Country Strategy." March. www.state.gov/wp-content/uploads/2022/05/ICS_EAP_Taiwan_Public.pdf.

Anadolu Agency. 2023. "China Denounces German Lawmakers' Visit to Taiwan." January 9. www.aa.com.tr/en/asia-pacific/china-denounces-german-lawmakers-visit-to-taiwan/2783029.

Aspen Institute. 2023. *Fireside Chat with Emmanuel Bonne*. www.youtube.com/live/DO1yVJZ83hY?feature=share&t=759.

Associated Press. 2022. "China on Taiwan: 'External Interference' Won't Be Tolerated." September 24. www.politico.com/news/2022/09/24/china-taiwan-united-nations-00058714.

Atkinson, Joel. 2013. *Australia and Taiwan: Bilateral Relations, China, the United States, and the South Pacific*. Boston: Brill.

Auswärtiges Amt. 2022. "Erklärungen." August 3. www.auswaertiges-amt.de/de/newsroom/-/2545960.

Bōeishō. 2021. "Bōei Hakusho." www.mod.go.jp/j/publication/wp/wp2021/pdf/wp2021_JP_Full.pdf.

Borrell, Josep. 2023a. "My View on China and EU-China Relations." *EEAS* (blog). April 13. www.eeas.europa.eu/eeas/my-view-china-and-eu-china-relations_en.

———. 2023b. "Speech by High Representative/Vice-President Josep Borrell on EU-China Relations." EEAS. April 18. www.eeas.europa.eu/eeas/ep-plenary-speech-high-representativevice-president-josep-borrell-eu-china-relations_en.

———. 2023c. "Un Regard Froid Sur La Chine." *EEAS* (blog). April 23. www.eeas.europa.eu/eeas/un-regard-froid-sur-la-chine_und_fr.

Bloomberg. 2024a. "Xi, Biden and the $10 Trillion Cost of War Over Taiwan." January 9. www.bloomberg.com/news/features/2024-01-09/if-china-invades-taiwan-it-would-cost-world-economy-10-trillion.

Bloomberg. 2024b. "U.S. Spies See China, Russia Militaries Working Closer on Taiwan." May 2. www.bloomberg.com/news/articles/2024-05-02/us-spies-see-china-russia-militaries-working-closer-on-taiwan.

Brown, Scott A. W. 2022. "Fraying at the Edges: A Subsystems/Normative Power Analysis of the EU's 'One China Policy/Policies.'" *China Quarterly* 252: 1001–24. https://doi.org/10.1017/S0305741022001345.

Bundesregierung. 2021. "Koalitionsvertrag." www.bundesregierung.de/breg-de/aktuelles/koalitionsvertrag-2021-1990800.

———. 2022. "Federal Chancellor Scholz on His Inaugural Visit to China." November 4. www.bundesregierung.de/breg-en/news/federal-chancellor-in-china-2140012.

Bureau Français de Taipei. 2023. "Faguo Zai Taiwan Yiti Shang Weichi Yizhi de Lichang ... " Facebook. April 11.

Bush, Richard C. 2004. *At Cross Purposes: U.S.-Taiwan Relations since 1942*. Armonk, NY: M.E. Sharpe.

———. 2017. *A One-China Policy Primer*. Washington, DC: Brookings Institution. www.brookings.edu/wp-content/uploads/2017/03/one-china-policy-primer.pdf.

Cabestan, Jean-Pierre. 2001. "France's Taiwan Policy: A Case of Shopkeeper Diplomacy." Paper presented at conference on "The Role of France and Germany in Sino-European Relations." Hong Kong Baptist University. www.sciencespo.fr/ceri/sites/sciencespo.fr.ceri/files/jpcabest.pdf.

Cabinet. 1969. "Implementation of Canadian China Policy." January 30. https://recherche-collection-search.bac-lac.gc.ca/eng/home/record?app=cabcon&IdNumber=2757.

Campbell, Kurt M., and Jake Sullivan. 2019. "Competition Without Catastrophe." *Foreign Affairs*. www.foreignaffairs.com/articles/china/competition-with-china-without-catastrophe.

"Canadian Trade Office in Taipei, Taiwan." 2022. Global Affairs Canada. February 28. www.international.gc.ca/country-pays/taiwan/taipei.aspx?lang=eng.

CBS News. 2022. "President Joe Biden." September 18. www.cbsnews.com/news/president-joe-biden-taiwan-60-minutes-2022-09-18/.

Chen, Wenshou. 2008. "'Zhengjing fenli' yu taihan guanxi – 'sanying guanxi' zhi mosuo." *Aisixiang*, January. www.aisixiang.com/data/17299.html.

Chen, Yu-Jie. 2022. "'One China' Contention in China–Taiwan Relations: Law, Politics and Identity." *The China Quarterly* 252: 1025–44. https://doi.org/10.1017/S0305741022001333.

Chiang, Frank. 2017. *The One-China Policy: State, Sovereignty, and Taiwan's International Legal Status*. Amsterdam: Elsevier.

China.org.cn. 2004. "Partnerschaft in Globaler Verantwortung." May 2004. http://german.china.org.cn/german/237912.htm.

Cho, Hyun-gyu. 2021. "jungguki daemaneul muryeokeuro tongilhaneun se gaji jogeon." August 2. http://timesisa.com/m/content/view.html?section=112&category=114&no=30231.

Christopher, Warren. 1996. "American Interests and the U.S.-China Relationship." U.S. Department of State. May 17. https://1997-2001.state.gov/current/debate/96517qa.html.

CIA.gov. 2023. "Director Burns' Remarks at the Aspen Security Forum." July 21. www.cia.gov/stories/story/director-burns-remarks-at-the-aspen-security-forum-2023/.

CNN. 2023. "North Korea a 'clear and Present Danger,' Says South Korean Foreign Minister." February 23. https://edition.cnn.com/2023/02/22/asia/south-korea-foreign-minister-interview-intl-hnk/index.html.

——— 2023. "Fareed Zakaria GPS (Transcript)." June 4. https://transcripts.cnn.com/show/fzgps/date/2023-06-04/segment/01.

CRS. 2015. "China/Taiwan: Evolution of the 'One China' Policy." Congressional Research Service.

Department of State. 2022. "U.S. Relations with Taiwan." May 28.

Der Spiegel 2004. "Bundesregierung warnt Taiwan." May 3. www.spiegel.de/politik/ausland/china-politik-bundesregierung-warnt-taiwan-a-298231.html.

Deutscher Bundestag. 2019. "Öffentliche Sitzung des Petitionsausschusses." December 9. www.bundestag.de/webarchiv/Ausschuesse/ausschuesse19/a02/anhoerung-9-12-19-672888.

DFAT. 2020. "Joint Statement Australia-U.S. Ministerial Consultations (AUSMIN)." Department of Foreign Affairs and Trade. www.dfat.gov.au/geo/united-states-of-america/ausmin/joint-statement-ausmin-2020.

——— 2023a. "AUKMIN Joint Statement." DFAT. www.dfat.gov.au/countries-economies-and-regions/2023-aukmin-joint-statement.

——— 2023b. "Australian Interests in a Regional Balance of Power." Minister for Foreign Affairs. April 17. www.foreignminister.gov.au/minister/penny-wong/speech/national-press-club-address-australian-interests-regional-balance-power.

Doran, Stuart, and David Lee, eds. 2002. *Australia and Recognition of the People's Republic of China, 1949–1972*. Documents on Australian Foreign Policy. Canberra: Dept. of Foreign Affairs and Trade. http://books.google.com/books?id=pMJyAAAAMAAJ.

Drian, Jean-Yves Le. 2021. "Déclaration." vie-publique.fr. June 8. www.vie-publique.fr/discours/280354-jean-yves-le-drian-08062021-france-taiwan.

Drun, Jessica, and Bonnie Glaser. 2022. *The Distortion of UN Resolution 2758 to Limit Taiwan's Access to the United Nations*. Washington, DC: GMF.

DW. 2019. "Taiwan-Petition im Bundestag." December 9. www.dw.com/de/petition-macht-taiwan-zum-thema-im-bundestag/a-51600818.

Editorial Board. 2023. "What Is the Future of the War in Ukraine? NATO's Leader Offers Insight." *Washington Post*, May 9. www.washingtonpost.com/opinions/2023/05/09/interview-jens-stoltenberg-nato-ukraine/.

EEAS. 2021a. "The European Union and Taiwan." European Economic and Trade Office in Taiwan. July 26. www.eeas.europa.eu/delegations/taiwan/european-union-and-taiwan_en?s=242.

2021b "Who we are." European Economic and Trade Office in Taiwan. July 26. www.eeas.europa.eu/delegations/taiwan/who-we-are_en?s=242.

Election Study Center. 2024. "Zhongyao zhengzhi taidu fenbu qushitu." July 8. https://esc.nccu.edu.tw/PageDoc/Detail?fid=7280&id=6528.

European Commission. 1994. "Towards a New Asia Strategy." https://eur-lex.europa.eu/legal-content/EN/ALL/?uri=CELEX:51994DC0314.

2006. "EU-China: Closer Partners, Growing Responsibilities."

2016. "Elements for a New EU Strategy on China." https://eeas.europa.eu/archives/docs/china/docs/joint_communication_to_the_european_parliament_and_the_council_-_elements_for_a_new_eu_strategy_on_china.pdf.

2019. "EU-China – A Strategic Outlook." https://ec.europa.eu/commission/sites/beta-political/files/communication-eu-china-a-strategic-outlook.pdf.

2021. "The EU Strategy for Cooperation in the Indo-Pacific." www.eeas.europa.eu/sites/default/files/jointcommunication_2021_24_1_en.pdf.

European Council. 2023. "Conclusions." https://data.consilium.europa.eu/doc/document/ST-7-2023-INIT/en/pdf.

European Parliament. 2019. "Verbatim Report of Proceedings." January 30. www.europarl.europa.eu/doceo/document/CRE-8-2019-01-30-ITM-022_EN.html.

2021. "EU-Taiwan Relations: MEPs Push for Stronger Partnership." October 21. www.europarl.europa.eu/news/en/press-room/20211014IPR14926/eu-taiwan-relations-meps-push-for-stronger-partnership.

Evans, Gareth. 1989. "Asia-Pacific: An Australian View." *Australian Foreign Affairs and Trade* 60 (6): 280–83.

Federal Government. 2022. "Progress Report Indo-Pacific 2022." www.aus waertiges-amt.de/blob/2551720/02b94659532c6af17e40a831bed8fe57/ 220906-fortschrittsbericht-der-indo-pazifik-leitlinien-data.pdf.

Financial Times. 2022. "NATO Holds First Dedicated Talks on China Threat to Taiwan Transatlantic Security Body Discussed How to Make Beijing Aware of Consequences of Any Military Action." November 30. https://www.ft.com/content/d7fa2d2b-53be-4175-bf2b-92af5defa622.

———. 2024. "Taiwan's Top Security Officials Make Secret Trip to US for Talks." August 22. https://www.ft.com/content/c4c5f7b3-9506-422b-a892-7b89e90a1631.

Focus Taiwan. 2023. "Taiwan Foreign Minister Meets EU Parliamentarians in Brussels." June 17. https://focustaiwan.tw/politics/202306170005.

Fōkasu Taiwan. 2024. "Nikkakon Chairman Furuya: Japan-Taiwan Trust 'Extremely Deep'; Attends Presidential Inauguration." May 20. https://japan.focustaiwan.tw/politics/202405200008.

Foreign Office. 2023. "Germany and Taiwan: Bilateral Relations." March 21. www.auswaertiges-amt.de/en/aussenpolitik/laenderinformationen/taiwan-node/taiwan/233988.

France 24. 2021. "French Senator Calls Taiwan a 'country' in Visit China Protests," July 10. www.france24.com/en/live-news/20211007-french-senator-calls-taiwan-a-country-in-visit-china-protests.

Frolic, B. Michael. 2022. *Canada and China: A Fifty-Year Journey.* Toronto: University of Toronto Press. Kindle Edition.

FRG. 2023. "Strategy on China." Federal Foreign Office. www.auswaertiges-amt.de/blob/2608580/49d50fecc479304c3da2e2079c55e106/china-strategie-en-data.pdf.

Fujita, Naotaka. 2021. "Taiwan mondai no 'heiwateki kaiketsu.'" *Asahi Shimbun,* May 24.

Fukuda, Madoka. 2012. "The Normalization of Sino-French Diplomatic Relations in 1964 and the Formation of the 'One-China' Principle." *World Political Science* 8(1): 252–71.

G7. 2021a. "Foreign and Development Ministers' Meeting: Communiqué." May 5 www.gov.uk/government/publications/g7-foreign-and-development-ministers-meeting-may-2021-communique/g7-foreign-and-development-ministers-meeting-communique-london-5-may-2021.

———. 2021b. "Summit Communique." GOV.UK. July 12. www.gov.uk/government/publications/carbis-bay-g7-summit-communique.

———. 2022. "Foreign Ministers' Statement on Preserving Peace and Stability Across the Taiwan Strait." www.auswaertiges-amt.de/en/newsroom/news/-/2545896.

    2023a. "Foreign Ministers' Communiqué." www.diplomatie.gouv.fr/en/french-foreign-policy/global-challenges/news/article/g7-japan-2023-foreign-ministers-communique-april-18-2023.

    2023b. "Hiroshima Leaders' Communiqué." www.mofa.go.jp/files/100506878.pdf.

Gaimushō. 1972. "Nicchū Kyōdō Seimei." September 29. www.mofa.go.jp/mofaj/area/china/nc_seimei.html.

    2023a. "Gaikō Seisho." www.mofa.go.jp/mofaj/gaiko/bluebook/2023/pdf/index.html.

    2023b. "Déclaration Conjointe." www.mofa.go.jp/files/100502056.pdf.

Haiguan Zongshu. 2023. "2022nian 12yue Jinchukou Shangpin Zhiyao Guobie." Zhonghua Renmin Gongheguo Haiguan Zhongshu. January 13. www.customs.gov.cn/customs/302249/zfxxgk/2799825/302274/302275/4794352/index.html.

Hansard. 1955a. "Formosa and the Pescadores (Treaties)." May 4. https://api.parliament.uk/historic-hansard/written-answers/1955/feb/04/formosa-and-the-pescadores-treaties.

    1955b. "Far East (Formosa and the Pescadores)." May 4. https://api.parliament.uk/historic-hansard/commons/1955/may/04/far-east-formosa-and-the-pescadores.

    1972. "China (Exchange of Ambassadors)." March 13. https://api.parliament.uk/historic-hansard/commons/1972/mar/13/china-exchange-of-ambassadors.

Helmke, Gretchen, and Steven Levitsky. 2003. "Informal Institutions and Comparative Politics: A Research Agenda." Working Paper. Kellogg Institute For International Studies. https://kellogg.nd.edu/documents/1600.

Hirakawa, Sachiko. 2006. "'Futatsu No Chugoku' Jirenma Kaiketsu e No Gaiko Wakugumi." *Kokusai Seiji* 146: 140–55.

HM Government. 2023. "Integrated Review Refresh 2023." https://assets.publishing.service.gov.uk/government/uploads/system/uploads/attachment_data/file/1145586/11857435_NS_IR_Refresh_2023_Supply_AllPages_Revision_7_WEB_PDF.pdf.

House of Commons (Canada). 1970. *House of Commons Debates (Third Session-Twenty-Eighth Parliament)*. Vol. 1. Ottawa: Queen's Printer for Canada. https://parl.canadiana.ca/view/oop.debates_HOC2803_01/51.

House of Commons (UK). 2023. *Tilting Horizons: The Integrated Review and the Indo-Pacific*. London: Foreign Affairs Committee.

Hsiao, Frank S. T., and Lawrence R. Sullivan. 1979. "The Chinese Communist Party and the Status of Taiwan, 1928–1943." *Pacific Affairs* 52(3): 446–67. https://doi.org/10.2307/2757657.

ITA. 2023. "Taiwan-South Korea Economic Relations." Text. MOEA. International Trade Administration, MOEA. February 2. www.trade.gov.tw/english/BilateralTrade/BilateralTrade.aspx?code=7030&nodeID=4639#.

Juppé, Alain. 1993. "Diplomatie Française : Le Deuxième Souffle." *Politique Internationale* 61: 13–32.

Kishida, Fumio, and Jens Stoltenberg. 2023. "Joint Statement." NATO. January 31. www.nato.int/cps/en/natohq/opinions_211294.htm.

Korea Times. 2024. "Taiwan calls on Korea and like-minded nations to help fight off China's threats." October 24. www.koreatimes.co.kr/www/nation/2024/06/113_361704.html.

Klintworth, Gary. 1993. *Australia's Taiwan Policy, 1942–1992*. Canberra: Australian National University. http://catalog.hathitrust.org/api/volumes/oclc/30058116.html.

Kyodo. 2023a. "Ex-Japan PM Taro Aso Says Japan, U.S. Must Resolve to Fight for Taiwan," August 8. https://english.kyodonews.net/news/2023/08/08f4020c9bcc-ex-japan-pm-aso-says-japan-us-must-resolve-to-fight-for-taiwan.html.

———. 2023b. "Japan Dispatched Civilian Defense Official to Taiwan in Spring," September 13. Access World News.

Lawrence, Susan. 2024. "Taiwan: Background and U.S. Relations." Congressional Research Service. https://crsreports.congress.gov/product/pdf/IF/IF10275.

Lee, Chaewon, and Adam P. Liff. 2023. "Reassessing Seoul's 'One China' Policy: South Korea-Taiwan 'Unofficial' Relations after 30 Years (1992–2022)." *Journal of Contemporary China* 32 (143): 745–64. https://doi.org/10.1080/10670564.2022.2113959.

Lee, Sang-Ock. 2003. *Jeonhwangui Hanguk Oegyo: Yi Sang-Ock Jeonoemujanggwan Oegyohoegorok*. Seoul: Samgwakkum.

Le Monde. 2024. "Entre La France et La Chine, Soixante Ans de Relations Diplomatiques Tumultueuses et Déséquilibrées." May 5. https://www.lemonde.fr/international/article/2024/05/05/entre-la-france-et-la-chine-soixante-ans-de-relations-diplomatiques-tumultueuses-et-desequilibrees_6231644_3210.html.

Leyen, Ursula von der. 2023. "Statement." Text. European Commission. May 19. https://ec.europa.eu/commission/presscorner/detail/en/statement_23_2824.

Libération. 2022. "Ce Que Nous Défendons En Aidant l'Ukraine, c'est Notre Propre Sécurité." August 5. https://www.liberation.fr/international/europe/catherine-colonna-ministre-des-affaires-etrangeres-ce-que-nous-defendons-en-aidant-lukraine-cest-notre-propre-securite-20220804_7OHWT7XRZNAHNAWVQA2OP6J7IM/.

Liff, Adam P. 2022a. "The U.S.-Japan Alliance and Taiwan." *Asia Policy* 29 (3): 125–60. https://doi.org/10.1353/asp.2022.0038.

— 2022b. "Japan, Taiwan and the 'One China' Framework after 50 Years." *The China Quarterly* 252: 1066–93. https://doi.org/10.1017/S0305741022001357.

— 2024. "How Japan and South Korea Diverge on Taiwan and the Taiwan Strait,'" *Brookings Institution*, February 22. www.brookings.edu/articles/how-japan-and-south-korea-diverge-on-taiwan-and-the-taiwan-strait/.

Liff, Adam P., and Dalton Lin. 2022. "The 'One China' Framework at 50 (1972–2022): The Myth of 'Consensus' and Its Evolving Policy Significance." *The China Quarterly* 252: 977–1000. https://doi.org/10.1017/S030574102200131X.

Lin, Bonny, Brian Hart, Samantha Lu, Hannah Price, and Matthew Slade. 2023. "Putting Taiwan President Tsai Ing-Wen's 2023 U.S. Transit in Context." *ChinaPower Project* (blog). March 27. https://chinapower.csis.org/taiwan-president-tsai-ing-wen-transit-united-states/.

MacKerras, Colin. 2000. "Australia–China Relations at the End of the Twentieth Century." *Australian Journal of International Affairs* 54(2): 185–200. https://doi.org/10.1080/713613512.

Mainichi Shimbun. 2023. "Taiwan yuji, Nichibei ga sakusen keikaku," January 3.

Martin, Garret. 2008. "Playing the China Card?: Revisiting France's Recognition of Communist China, 1963–1964." Journal of Cold War Studies 10(1): 52–80.

Mastro, Oriana Skylar, and Sungmin Cho. 2022. "How South Korea Can Contribute to the Defense of Taiwan." *The Washington Quarterly* 45(3): 109–29.

Matsuda, Yasuhiro. 2020. "Anteika suru ChuTai Kankei shita de tenkai suru NitTai Kankei: 2008-16nen." In *NitTai Kankeishi: 1945–2020*, edited by Kawashima Shin, Shimizu Urara, Matsuda Yasuhiro, and Yang Yongming. Tokyo Daigaku Shuppansha.

McGregor, Richard. 2023. "Australia's Caution on Taiwan May Not Last." Brookings. March 29. www.brookings.edu/articles/australias-caution-on-taiwan-may-not-last/.

MEFA. 2022. "France's Indo-Pacific Strategy." Paris: Ministry for Europe and Foreign Affairs.
———. 2023. "Joint Statement." Ministry for Europe and Foreign Affairs. January 30. www.diplomatie.gouv.fr/en/country-files/australia/news/article/joint-statement-second-france-australia-foreign-and-defence-ministerial.
Mengin, Françoise. 1997. "Taiwan's Non-official Diplomacy." *Diplomacy & Statecraft* 8 (1): 228–48. https://doi.org/10.1080/09592299708406036.
———. 2002. "A Functional Relationship: Political Extensions to Europe-Taiwan Economic Ties." *The China Quarterly*, (169): 136–53.
MFA(PRC). 2020. "Waijiaobu fayanren Geng Shuang jiu youguan guojia gaoguan huhe Taiwan diqu xuanjushi da jizhe wen". January 12. https://web.archive.org/web/20200509132316/https://www.fmprc.gov.cn/web/fyrbt_673021/dhdw_673027/t1731294.shtml.
MFA (PRC). 2023. "Wang Yi Meets with U.S. Secretary of State Antony Blinken." June 19. www.fmprc.gov.cn/mfa_eng/zxxx_662805/202306/t20230619_11099852.html.
MFA(PRC). 2004. "Joint Statement of the 7th China-EU Summit." MFA(PRC). December 9. www.fmprc.gov.cn/eng/wjdt_665385/2649_665393/200412/t20041209_679122.html.
———. 2022. "Statement." www.fmprc.gov.cn/eng/wjdt_665385/2649_665393/202208/t20220802_10732293.html.
Ministère des Affaires étrangères. 1994. "Communiqué conjoint franco-chinois." January 12. www.vie-publique.fr/discours/133004-communique-conjoint-franco-chinois-en-date-du-12-janvier-1994-sur-le-r.
Ministère de l'Europe et des Affaires étrangères. 2023. "Chine – Q&R – Extrait Du Point de Presse." April 13. www.diplomatie.gouv.fr/fr/dossiers-pays/chine/evenements/article/chine-q-r-extrait-du-point-de-presse-13-04-23.
Ministry of Economic Affairs. 2023. "Taiwan-Japan Economic Relations." Bureau of Foreign Trade. February 16. www.trade.gov.tw/english/BilateralTrade/BilateralTrade.aspx?code=7030&nodeID=4639.
MOFA(ROC). 2022. "Relations Taiwan-France." October 6. https://roc-taiwan.org/fr_fr/post/15.html.
"National Strategic Review." 2022. Secrétariat général de la défense et de la sécurité nationale. www.sgdsn.gouv.fr/files/files/rns-uk-20221202.pdf.
NATO. 1949. "The North Atlantic Treaty." NATO. www.nato.int/cps/en/natohq/official_texts_17120.htm.
———. 2019. "London Declaration." NATO. December 4. www.nato.int/cps/en/natohq/official_texts_171584.htm.

2022. "2022 Strategic Concept." www.nato.int/nato_static_fl2014/assets/pdf/2022/6/pdf/290622-strategic-concept.pdf.

2023. "Conversation." NATO. May 15. www.nato.int/cps/en/natohq/opinions_214381.htm.

Naval News. 2024. "German Navy Ships Transit Taiwan Strait, Draw Chinese Criticism." September 16. www.navalnews.com/naval-news/2024/09/german-navy-transits-taiwan-strait/.

NEAR. 2023. *The Impact of Xi Jinping's New Era on Korea and the World*. Seoul: Northeast Asia Research Foundation.

New York Times. 1950. "Texts of Statements on China." January 7. www.nytimes.com/1950/01/07/archives/texts-of-statements-on-china-text-of-yehs-statement.html.

1964. "France Forces Taiwan to Break Diplomatic Ties." February 11. www.nytimes.com/1964/02/11/archives/france-forces-taiwan-to-break-diplomatic-ties-taipei-acts-after.html.

1969. "The Nixon-Sato Communique." November 22. www.nytimes.com/1969/11/22/archives/the-nixonsato-communique.html.

1994. "France Bars Taiwan Sales, Warming China Ties." January 13.

Nikkei Asia. 2021. "Taiwan Conflict Would 'trash' World Economy: Kurt Campbell." May 5. https://asia.nikkei.com/Politics/International-relations/US-China-tensions/Taiwan-conflict-would-trash-world-economy-Kurt-Campbell.

2023. "NATO Chief Says China Has 'no Justification' for Taiwan Threats." February 1. https://asia.nikkei.com/Editor-s-Picks/Interview/NATO-chief-says-China-has-no-justification-for-Taiwan-threats.

Park, Cheol-hee. 2022. "Daeman Munjeneun Gang Geonneo Bul-i Anida." Www.Seoul.Co.Kr/, December 18. www.seoul.co.kr/news/newsView.php?id=20221219027014.

Pew. 2023. "China's Approach to Foreign Policy Gets Largely Negative Reviews in 24-Country Survey." July 27. www.pewresearch.org/global/2023/07/27/chinas-approach-to-foreign-policy-gets-largely-negative-reviews-in-24-country-survey/.

Politico. 2023. "Germany's Sharp-Tongued Annalena Baerbock Rips up the Diplomatic Playbook," April 24. www.politico.eu/article/annalena-baerbock-germany-rip-diplomatic-playbook/.

PRC Embassy Japan. 2024. "Zainichi Chūgoku taishikan ga 'Taiwan mondai to Chūnichi kankei' zadankai kaisai." May 23. http://jp.china-embassy.gov.cn/jpn/dsgxx/202405/t20240523_11310534.htm.

Ratner, Ely. 2021. "Statement." Committee on Foreign Relations United States Senate, December 8. https://www.foreign.senate.gov/imo/media/doc/120821_Ratner_Testimony1.pdf.

Reilly, Michael. 2020. *The Great Free Trade Myth: British Foreign Policy and East Asia Since 1980*. Singapore: Springer. https://doi.org/10.1007/978-981-15-8558-6.

Renmin Ribao. 2023. "Zhengque Yindao Minying Jingji Jiankang Fazhan Gao Zhiliang Fazhan." March 7. www.news.cn/politics/leaders/2023-03/06/c_1129417096.htm.

Reuters. 2007. "France Opposes Taiwan Referendum: Sarkozy." November 26. www.reuters.com/article/us-china-france-taiwan/france-opposes-taiwan-referendum-sarkozy-idUST30639920071126.

———. 2018. "Germany's Schroeder Warns against Demonizing China." November 16. www.reuters.com/article/us-germany-china-schroeder-idUKKCN1NL1UM.

———. 2021a. "U.S. and Allies Would 'take Action' If Taiwan Attacked – Blinken." November 10. www.reuters.com/world/asia-pacific/us-allies-would-take-action-if-taiwan-attacked-blinken-2021-11-10/.

———. 2021b. "Silent Partners." November 29. www.reuters.com/investigates/special-report/taiwan-china-submarines/.

———. 2023a. "Germany Will Not Arm Taiwan, Senior Lawmaker Says." January 11. www.usnews.com/news/world/articles/2023-01-11/germany-will-not-arm-taiwan-senior-lawmaker-says.

———. 2023b. "Macron: France Favours 'status Quo' on Taiwan, Position Unchanged." April 12. www.reuters.com/world/china/macron-france-favours-status-quo-taiwan-position-unchanged-2023-04-12/.

———. 2023c. "Germany's Scholz: I Warned China on Using Force against Taiwan." June 22, 2023, sec. World. www.reuters.com/world/germanys-scholz-i-warned-china-using-force-against-taiwan-2023-06-22/.

———. 2023d. "UK Approves Increased Submarine-Related Exports to Taiwan, Risking Angering China." March 14. www.reuters.com/world/uk/uk-approves-increased-submarine-related-exports-taiwan-risking-angering-china-2023-03-13/.

———. 2023e. "UK Security Minister Breaks with Convention to Meet Taiwanese Minister." June 16. www.reuters.com/world/uk-security-minister-breaks-with-convention-meet-taiwanese-minister-sources-2023-06-16/.

———. 2024. "US Military, Seeking Strategic Advantages, Builds Up Australia's Northern Bases Amid China Tensions." July 26. www.reuters.com/world/taiwanese-minister-make-rare-britain-visit-this-week-2023–06-11.

RFI. 2021. "French Senate's Taiwan Vote Triggers Beijing's Anger Again." May 7. www.rfi.fr/en/international/20210507-french-senate-s-taiwan-vote-triggers-beijing-s-anger-again.

ROK Government. 2022. *Strategy for a Free, Peaceful, and Prosperous Indo-Pacific Region*. Seoul: Republic of Korea.

Romberg, Alan D. 2003. *Rein In at the Brink of the Precipice: American Policy Toward Taiwan and U.S.-PRC Relations*. Washington, DC: Stimson Center. www.stimson.org/2001/rein-brink-precipice-american-policy-toward-taiwan-and-us-prc-relations/.

Schubert, Gunter. 2001. "The European Dimension of German-Taiwanese Relations – A Critical Assessment." *Les Dossiers Du CERI*, June 23. https://www.sciencespo.fr/ceri/sites/sciencespo.fr.ceri/files/schubert.pdf.

Shimizu, Urara. 2020. "'Ushinawareta koki' to shinka suru tsumiageshiki jitsumu kankei." In *NitTai Kankeishi: 1945–2020*, edited by Kawashima Shin, Shimizu Urara, Matsuda Yasuhiro, and Yang Yongming, 259–279. Tokyo Daigaku Shuppansha.

Shin, Chueiling. 2001. "Development of ROC-France Relations: The Case of an Isolated State and Its Economic Diplomacy." *Issues & Studies* 37(1): 124–59.

Simon, Scott. 2023. "The Taiwan Strait: What Can Canada Do?" *CDA Institute Threat Assessment* 1: 1–11.

Sinha, Rohan, and Stefan Talmon. 2019. "Germany Confirms Non-Recognition of the Republic of China (Taiwan)." *German Practice in International Law* (blog). December 18. https://gpil.jura.uni-bonn.de/2019/12/germany-confirms-non-recognition-of-the-republic-of-china-taiwan/.

Slovenian Presidency of the EU. 2008. "Declaration by the Presidency on Behalf of the European Union on Cross-Strait Relations." March 22. www.eu2008.si/en/News_and_Documents/CFSP_Statements/March/0322MZZ_Tajvan.html.

Soames, Christopher. 1975. "Speech by Sir Christopher Soames." Strasbourg, June 18. http://aei.pitt.edu/8484/.

Somers, Werner. 2023. *The State of Taiwan*. Leiden, The Netherlands: Brill.

South China Morning Post. 2023. "South Korean Lawmaker Feuds with Beijing over Taiwan Trip Protest," January 6. www.scmp.com/news/asia/east-asia/article/3205820/lawmaker-accuses-beijing-interference-south-koreas-internal-affairs-amid-anger-over-parliamentary.

State Council. 1993. "The Taiwan Question and Reunification of China." www.jstor.org/stable/30172771.

2022. "The Taiwan Question and China's Reunification in the New Era." August 2022. http://us.china-embassy.gov.cn/eng/zgyw/202208/t20220810_10740168.htm.

@StateDeptSpox. 2022. Tweet. *Twitter.* https://twitter.com/StateDeptSpox/status/1527823885600755714.

Stilwell, David R. 2020. "Remarks." American Institute in Taiwan. August 31. www.ait.org.tw/remarks-by-david-r-stilwell-assistant-secretary-of-state-for-east-asian-and-pacific-affairs-at-the-heritage-foundation-virtual/.

Taipei Times. 2011. "Seoul pulling plug on military exchange." May 5. www.taipeitimes.com/News/front/archives/2011/05/05/2003502436.

2022. "Strait Belongs to All: Top French Officer." July 11. www.taipeitimes.com/News/front/archives/2022/07/11/2003781531.

2023. "Joseph Wu Meets with Italy Lawmakers." June 19. www.taipeitimes.com/News/front/archives/2023/06/19/2003801756.

"Taiwan Relations Act." 1979. American Institute in Taiwan. January 1. www.ait.org.tw/our-relationship/policy-history/key-u-s-foreign-policy-documents-region/taiwan-relations-act/.

Taiwanreporter. 2018. "Und Taiwan? Bundesregierung definiert ihre Ein-China-Politik." August 16. www.youtube.com/watch?v=fL_Vt102vSY.

Taiwan Today. 2023. "MOFA Welcomes Visit by Australian Parliamentary Delegation." September 26. https://taiwantoday.tw/news.php?unit=2&post=242506.

TBS. 2021. "Suga Shushō ' Hatsu ' No Tōshu Tōron." Youtube. June 9. www.youtube.com/watch?v=dv1CTKUdSI4.

The Guardian. 2021. "Scott Morrison Accidentally Endorses Beijing Position." May 6. https://amp.theguardian.com/australia-news/2021/may/06/scott-morrison-accidentally-endorses-beijing-policy-for-taiwan-in-foreign-policy-blunder?__twitter_impression=true&s=09.

2022a. "Chinese Ambassador Warns UK Not to Cross 'Red Lines' over Taiwan." August 16. www.theguardian.com/world/2022/aug/16/chinese-ambassador-warns-uk-not-to-cross-red-lines-over-taiwan.

2022b. "Rishi Sunak Calls China 'Systemic Challenge', in Sign of Softer UK Stance." November 15. www.theguardian.com/politics/2022/nov/15/uk-china-rishi-sunak-g20-summit-bali.

Thümmel, Martin. 2022. "Taiwan: Opportunities and Challenges in Times of Geopolitical Change (Conference Recording)." Youtube. December 6. www.youtube.com/watch?v=aTrFoRWu8ow.

"Treaty of Peace and Friendship between Japan and the People's Republic of China." 1978. "The World and Japan" Database. August 12. https://worldjpn.net/documents/texts/docs/19780812.T1E.html.

"Treaty of Peace between Japan and the Republic of China." 1952. "The World and Japan" Database. April 28. https://worldjpn.net/documents/texts/docs/19520428.T1E.html.

"Treaty of Peace with Japan." 1951. UN. https://treaties.un.org/doc/publication/unts/volume%20136/volume-136-i-1832-english.pdf.

TRO UK. 2024. "Taiwan-UK Relations." Taipei Representative Office in the U.K. June 11. www.roc-taiwan.org/uk_en/post/39.html.

Tsai, Ing-wen. 2021. "President Tsai Delivers 2021 National Day Address." October 10. https://english.president.gov.tw/News/6175.

Tsang, Steve. 1994. "Unwitting Partners: Relations between Taiwan and Britain, 1950–1958." *East Asian History*, 105–20.

UK Parliament. 2020. "Taiwan." Hansard. July 14. https://hansard.parliament.uk/lords/2020-07-14/debates/33975CE2-BCAD-49BF-8F19-EFA195717BA1/Taiwan.

U*PI*. 2022. "Pelosi: Pentagon Worried China Would Shoot down Her Plane If She Visits Taiwan." July 22. www.upi.com/Top_News/World-News/2022/07/22/Nancy-Pelosi-Taiwan-warplane-shoot-down-visit/9431658470639/.

Vest, Charlie, Agatha Kratz, and Reva Goujon. 2022. "The Global Economic Disruptions from a Taiwan Conflict." *Rhodium Group* (blog). December 14. https://rhg.com/research/taiwan-economic-disruptions/.

Vestager, Margarethe. 2021. "EU-Taiwan Political Relations and Cooperation." EEAS. October 19. www.eeas.europa.eu/eeas/eu-taiwan-political-relations-and-cooperation-speech-behalf-high-representativevice-president_en.

Wachman, Alan M. 2007. *Why Taiwan?: Geostrategic Rationales for China's Territorial Integrity*. Stanford: Stanford University Press.

Wang, Yi. 2022. "ZhongMei Xin Shidai Zhengque Xiangchu Zhi Dao." Waijiaobu. September 23. www.fmprc.gov.cn/web/wjbz_673089/zyjh_673099/202209/t20220923_10770193.shtml.

Washington Post. 2022. "China Plans to Seize Taiwan on 'Much Faster Timeline,' Blinken Says," October 18. www.washingtonpost.com/world/2022/10/18/china-seize-taiwan-plan-blinken/.

White House. 2021a "Remarks by President Biden on America's Place in the World," February 5. www.whitehouse.gov/briefing-room/speeches-remarks/2021/02/04/remarks-by-president-biden-on-americas-place-in-the-world/.

2021b. "U.S.- Japan Joint Leaders' Statement." April 17. www.whitehouse.gov/briefing-room/statements-releases/2021/04/16/u-s-japan-joint-leaders-statement-u-s-japan-global-partnership-for-a-new-era/.

2021c. "U.S.-ROK Leaders' Joint Statement." May 21. www.whitehouse.gov/briefing-room/statements-releases/2021/05/21/u-s-rok-leaders-joint-statement/.

2022. "U.S.-Australia-Japan Trilateral Strategic Dialogue." August 5. www.state.gov/u-s-australia-japan-trilateral-strategic-dialogue/.

2023a. "Remarks by President Biden in a Press Conference." May 21. www.whitehouse.gov/briefing-room/speeches-remarks/2023/05/21/remarks-by-president-biden-in-a-press-conference/.

2023b. "The Spirit of Camp David." August 18. www.whitehouse.gov/briefing-room/statements-releases/2023/08/18/the-spirit-of-camp-david-joint-statement-of-japan-the-republic-of-korea-and-the-united-states/.

World Bank. 2024. "Germany Exports to China." June 28. https://wits.worldbank.org/CountryProfile/en/Country/DEU/StartYear/1988/EndYear/2021/TradeFlow/Export/Partner/CHN/Indicator/XPRT-TRD-VL.

Yomiuri. 2024. "Taiwan kaikyō tsūka." September 27.

Zhonghua Minguo Zongtongfu. 2020. "Zongtong jieshou yingguo guangbo gongsi zhuanfang neirong." January 18. https://www.president.gov.tw/NEWS/25191.

Zhonghua Minguo Zongtongfu. 2024. "Zongtong fabiao jiuzhi yanshuo." May 20. https://www.president.gov.tw/NEWS/28428.

Zhang, Xiaotong. 2014. "EU-China Economic Diplomacy: When Economics Meets Politics." Wuhan University Center for Economic Diplomacy. November 19. http://ced.whu.edu.cn/Show/?id=103&siteid=3.

Cambridge Elements

Politics and Society in East Asia

Erin Aeran Chung
Johns Hopkins University

Erin Aeran Chung is the Charles D. Miller Professor of East Asian Politics in the Department of Political Science at the Johns Hopkins University. She specializes in East Asian political economy, migration and citizenship, and comparative racial politics. She is the author of *Immigration and Citizenship in Japan* (Cambridge, 2010, 2014; Japanese translation, Akashi Shoten, 2012) and *Immigrant Incorporation in East Asian Democracies* (Cambridge, 2020). Her research has been supported by grants from the Academy of Korean Studies, the Japan Foundation, the Japan Foundation Center for Global Partnership, the Social Science Research Council, and the American Council of Learned Societies.

Mary Alice Haddad
Wesleyan University

Mary Alice Haddad is the John E. Andrus Professor of Government, East Asian Studies, and Environmental Studies at Wesleyan University. Her research focuses on democracy, civil society, and environmental politics in East Asia as well as city diplomacy around the globe. A Fulbright and Harvard Academy scholar, Haddad is author of *Effective Advocacy: Lessons from East Asia's Environmentalists* (MIT, 2021), *Building Democracy in Japan* (Cambridge, 2012), and *Politics and Volunteering in Japan* (Cambridge, 2007), and co-editor of *Greening East Asia* (University of Washington, 2021), and *NIMBY is Beautiful* (Berghahn Books, 2015). She has published in journals such as *Comparative Political Studies, Democratization, Journal of Asian Studies*, and *Nonprofit and Voluntary Sector Quarterly*, with writing for the public appearing in the *Asahi Shimbun*, the *Hartford Courant*, and the *South China Morning Post*.

Benjamin L. Read
University of California, Santa Cruz

Benjamin L. Read is a professor of Politics at the University of California, Santa Cruz. His research has focused on local politics in China and Taiwan, and he also writes about issues and techniques in comparison and field research. He is author of *Roots of the State: Neighborhood Organization and Social Networks in Beijing and Taipei* (Stanford, 2012), coauthor of *Field Research in Political Science: Practices and Principles* (Cambridge, 2015), and co-editor of *Local Organizations and Urban Governance in East and Southeast Asia: Straddling State and Society* (Routledge, 2009). His work has appeared in journals such as *Comparative Political Studies, Comparative Politics, the Journal of Conflict Resolution, the China Journal, the China Quarterly*, and *the Washington Quarterly*, as well as several edited books.

About the Series

The Cambridge Elements series on Politics and Society in East Asia offers original, multidisciplinary contributions on enduring and emerging issues in the dynamic region of East Asia by leading scholars in the field. Suitable for general readers and specialists alike, these short, peer-reviewed volumes examine common challenges and patterns within the region while identifying key differences between countries. The series consists of two types of contributions: 1) authoritative field surveys of established concepts and themes that offer roadmaps for further research; and 2) new research on emerging issues that challenge conventional understandings of East Asian politics and society. Whether focusing on an individual country or spanning the region, the contributions in this series connect regional trends with points of theoretical debate in the social sciences and will stimulate productive interchanges among students, researchers, and practitioners alike.

Cambridge Elements

Politics and Society in East Asia

Elements in the Series

Japan as a Global Military Power: New Capabilities, Alliance Integration, Bilateralism-Plus
Christopher W. Hughes

State and Social Protests in China
Yongshun Cai and Chih-Jou Jay Chen

The State and Capitalism in China
Margaret M. Pearson, Meg Rithmire and Kellee Tsai

Political Selection in China: Rethinking Foundations and Findings
Melanie Manion

Environmental Politics in East Asia
Mary Alice Haddad

Politics of the North Korean Diaspora
Sheena Chestnut Greitens

The Adaptability of the Chinese Communist Party
Martin K. Dimitrov

The Welfare State in East Asia
Joseph Wong

Refugee Policies in East Asia
Petrice R. Flowers

Authoritarian Survival and Leadership Succession in North Korea and Beyond
Edward Goldring and Peter Ward

Japan's New Industrial Policy
Gregory W. Noble

U.S. Allies and the Taiwan Strait
Adam P. Liff

A full series listing is available at: www.cambridge.org/EPEA

Printed by Integrated Books International,
United States of America